Passive Income Ideas And Home-Based Business Opportunities

55

Ways to Make

Money Online Analyzed

[2nd Edition]

By

Michael Ezeanaka

www.MichaelEzeanaka.com

Disclaimer

This publication is designed to provide competent and reliable information regarding the subject matter covered. However, it is sold with the understanding that the author is not engaged in rendering investment or other professional advice. Laws and practices often vary from state to state and country to country and if investment or other expert assistance is required, the services of a professional should be sought. The author specifically disclaims any liability that is incurred from the use or application of the contents of this book.

Table of Contents

Introduction

In this day and age, it has become much easier to generate passive income. The internet, in particular, has given birth to a plethora of opportunities that enable smart and business-minded people to earn significant profits with very limited work. The lure of generating passive income has never been stronger. The idea of earning an income while vacationing in the Virgin Islands is a truly attractive prospect. However, things are easier said than done. Just like any form of profit-oriented activity, you have to put in the time and the work before you can see a stream of passive income going your way.

A lot of people make the mistake of equating earning passive income with get-rich-quick schemes. I hope that you don't make the same mistake. This is why I've put together this guide about the most common ways on how to earn passive income. My intention is to help you decide if an opportunity is right for you or not. I also want to help you debunk the myths and misconceptions surrounding these income-generating methods. The information and analysis you will find in this book are based on facts and observable trends. I want to make sure that you are on the right direction when you finally decide to find a way to generate passive income.

I also highly recommend that you nurture the attributes of patience and determination when you pursue any of the methods discussed in this book. These are virtues you are going to need because most of the methods here won't deliver instant income. Most of the time, you have to build the business from the ground up. If you don't have patience, you will give up before you start reaping the rewards that you deserve. If you don't have determination, then one setback can easily break down your spirit. My suggestion is that you should look into your passive income journey with long-term goals.

Take your time. Don't rush things. If you don't achieve a goal, just sit back and try to understand what went wrong. What did you do? What didn't you do? Then do things all over again. Sooner or later, things will come into place. Once you start seeing the earnings roll in, just sit back once again and try to see how you can scale the earnings. This is what successful online entrepreneurs do. You should do the same.

Furthermore, all businesses are not equal. Some of the business opportunities covered in this book are by their very nature passive while others aren't – this is why a passivity grade is assigned to them to help you compare and contrast. However, every business can be made more passive by applying certain strategies. Where necessary, strategies that will help increase the passivity of the business are suggested.

Finally, please bare in mind **this guide is by no means a comprehensive analysis of 55 business opportunities.** As much as I would have loved to cover every minute detail of each business, it'll be difficult to achieve that without making this book unnecessarily long.

However, what you'll find herein is a **brief overview of 55 ways you can earn passive income, or at the very least, make money online**. The intention here is to help you quickly compare and contrast each business model, pick out the opportunities that interest you the most and then do further research on them. It's my sincere hope that what you'll discover in this book will bring you one step closer to achieving the financial freedom you deserve.

Without further ado, lets get right into it!

What is Passive Income?

There are various definitions of passive income but the most common one is this: "It is income that you earn even if you are not actively trying to earn it." You are still earning it even if you are mowing your lawn or if you are on vacation in the Bahamas. In short, it's income that goes to your bank account whether you actively work for it or not. Rental income is one of the most common examples of passive income. You own a piece of land that a farmer rents for $1000 a month. Whether you do anything or not to the property, you will still receive the $1000 at the end of every month.

Passive income has been around since the dawn of civilization. Tributes that tribesmen bring to their chiefs can be considered as passive income by the nature of the tributes. These are products or goods that the chiefs themselves didn't work on. They simply receive them after every harvest cycle. With that said, the concept of passive income has been around for centuries.

However, it has evolved with the times. Economic movements have given birth to dozens of other ways on how to generate passive income. For example, the current technological revolution has created online economies that allow people to earn significant amounts of passive income. Anyone can start a website, sign up with Amazon, promote Amazon products, and earn commissions from every sale. These commissions are considered as passive income.

Why Is Passive Income Important?

Passive income is very important in the sense that it allows people to achieve some sort of financial freedom while getting the chance to indulge in the things that they are passionate about. For example, with an alternative source of income, you can spend more time doing something you love like going to the beach to surf, going to the mountains to hike or spending quality time with your loved ones. It enables to you to earn money without having to work day in and day out for it. Of course, the importance of passive income largely depends on where you are coming from and what your goals are in pursuing it.

But the bottom line here is that passive income offers you an opportunity to earn good money with less work. It is hard work at first but you slowly unburden yourself from the work as your business and passive income stream grows. That's the beauty of it. It gets easier and easier with the passage of time provided that you are doing things the right way and that you are scaling your business with the right strategies. The work you have done yesterday will continue to benefit you in the coming days, weeks, months, or even years. This is especially true if you are running a content-based business that's hosted online.

To cut the story short, passive income is important to those who are looking for a good source of alternative income that requires minimal work. It's important to those who want to supplement their income from their 9 to 5 jobs. It's important to those who want more time to pursue their passions. It's important to those who want to build businesses that have the potential of completely replacing their income from their ordinary jobs.

Finally, having a good passive income base will make you less dependent on your job. If for any reason you were to lose your job, you'll still have peace of mind knowing you have other ways of making money – ways you can easily scale up to replace the income from your job. This means, you'll not be at the mercy of the economy (i.e. economic downturn and subsequent job losses) or your boss. You'll be in control of your financial life.

Success Mindset

The two most important virtues that you need to achieve success in generating passive income are patience and determination. If you have both of these attributes, then you have the ideal mindset required to achieve success. Majority of those who fail in generating passive income do so because they give up too easily or they get discouraged with the slightest setback. Make no mistakes. The opportunities discussed in this book are by no means get rich quick schemes. If you don't have patience and determination, then it will be very difficult for you to create a great source of passive income.

In the context of passive income, patience means sticking to your guns for weeks, months, or even years. You have to always remember that it will take time before you get to see meaningful returns on your investments. For example, let's say that you built a blog which you monetized with advertisements and affiliate products. You should not expect your blog to generate income right out of the bat. It takes time for the blog to attract and grow readers. Sometimes, for the first months, you are going to earn nothing. If you don't have patience and determination, it's so easy to get discouraged and just give up.

Taking Responsibility for Your Success and Failures

In your passive income journey, you are going to go through a lot of ups and downs, failures and successes. You should own up to these failures because it's the only way to learn from your mistakes. It's easier to find solutions to problems if you accept the fact that you are responsible in fixing them. You see, one of the most common reasons why many aspiring online entrepreneurs fail is that they play the blame game when things don't go their way. They blame everyone but themselves. They blame the freelance writers they hired. They blame the social media marketers running their social media campaigns. They blame their staff. They actually spend more time finding someone to blame than finding a solution to the problem that caused the failure.

In a nutshell, success and failure come hand in hand. It's not uncommon for beginners to encounter more failures than successes. What really matters is how you deal with the failures. Are you going to let them discourage you? Or are you going to use them as lessons to be smarter the second time around? In my experience, successful and determined entrepreneurs follow the latter route. You should do the same.

Having this book by your side will give you tremendous leverage and a good head start because you'll know which business opportunity suits you best and which to avoid. However, if you wish to further cut down your learning curve and reduce the number of mistakes you'll make, we advise working with a mentor – someone who has achieved success in what it is you're trying to do.

Bear in mind, the best mentors tend to be those who are not too far ahead of you as they will be able to better understand the challenges you're currently going through since it wasn't too long ago they went through the same challenges themselves.

Adopting an Abundance Mindset

When we say you should adopt an abundance mindset, we are urging you to stay optimistic and focus all your attention on the good things and positive things that are happening in your passive income journey. Everything you do should be geared towards achieving the abundance you envisioned when you started your passive income journey. Having this mindset will keep your efforts glued to your most important goals.

Adopting an abundance mindset also involves dealing with setbacks and learning from them. In most cases, it's about turning your weaknesses into strengths. You failed to sell products in your first weeks? This happens to almost everyone so don't let it get to you too much. A smart entrepreneur would look back at what he did or what he didn't do and go from there with renewed passion knowing that he's not going to make the same mistakes again.

Mapping Out a Course of Action

Goal setting and planning are two of the most important things you should do before you embark on a journey to earn passive income. In goal setting, you identify both your short-term and long-term goals. There should also be a corresponding time periods for your goals. For example, where do you envision yourself after six months of pursuing your goals? After setting your goals, you then proceed to mapping out a plan on how you are going to achieve them. You can call it the "master plan" or the "blueprint". What's important is that it should contain the course of action you are going to implement in your attempt to get to your goals.

To recap things, you are going to need patience and determination if you want to last long as an entrepreneur. Being patient and determined also means owning up to your failures and successes. It's also your responsibility to learn from these failures and ensure that you don't go through them ever again. To help you deal with failures and mistakes, you should adopt the abundance mindset. This mindset helps you in making the most out of your failures. This mindset helps you in turning strengths into weaknesses. And last but not the least, always see to it that you are being guided by a map or course of action. Without setting your goals and creating a blueprint on how to reach them, you are going to be blind going in. So set those goals and write a plan of action before you do anything else.

55 Online Businesses Analyzed

Let's now get into the meat of the matter. Discussed in the upcoming pages are 55 of the best strategies on how to generate passive income. Like I mentioned before, the word "passive" is relative and some of the business opportunities analyzed below are more passive than the other. However, every business can be made more passive by applying certain strategies. Where applicable, these strategies will be discussed.

That being said, in the coming pages, you'll learn about 55 business opportunities, and how you can increase your chances of being successful with them. Most of these businesses require minimal monetary investment, which means working hard, and working smart is what you need to get things done. You should take the time to analyze and understand every strategy and opportunity. You should also consider testing out the strategies to see which ones will work well for you.

Without further ado, let's get on with the first one!

Inspiration #1

"If you can dream it, you can do it."

Walt Disney

Business #1

Amazon Kindle Direct Publishing

If you think you are a good writer or you simply want to make money as a publisher then kindle publishing is an opportunity you might want to explore. There are thousands of people out there who are making a lot of money from Kindle Publishing. If they can, then you can as well. What's great about Kindle Publishing is that you have the flexibility to choose what to write. You can write fiction or non-fiction and short stories or full novels. Some people even publish magazine-type articles on the platform. What Kindle Publishing does is connect you with your target readers. It's the perfect platform for people who want to independently publish their works.

Kindle allows you to publish both ebooks and paperbacks. What's great about the platform is that you have control over your rights for the book and you get to set your own list prices. Furthermore, you can make changes on your books any time you want. As far as earnings are concerned, you can receive up to 70% in royalty from your book sales. For example, if you priced your ebook at $2.99 per download, your royalties will be $2.093 per ebook sold (excluding download fees). That may not look like much but it quickly adds up once your sales start to pick up. The 70% royalty applies to numerous countries with huge Amazon markets like the United States, United Kingdom, India, Italy, Japan, Mexico, Canada, Germany, France, Spain, Brazil, and Australia.

Basically, here's how you publish your ebook or paperback on the Amazon Kindle Direct Publishing platform:

1. Write a book yourself or hire a ghostwriter to write for you. You can hire ghostwriters from freelance sites like upwork.com or fiverr.com. Alternatively, you can pay writing companies like EwriterSolutions and TheUrbanWriters to do the job for you.

2. Prepare your manuscript and cover. You can use Amazon's in-house tools and resources to complete this process. With regards to cover design, you can hire freelancers from fiverr to take care of this for as little as $5. Alternatively, you can design the cover yourself for free using the resources available at Canva.com

3. See to it that your manuscript meets the quality and content guidelines as put forth by Amazon. If you have the budget for it, try seeking the help of a professional editor and proof reader on upwork.com, fiverr.com or any other suitable website.

4. Sign up with KDP. If you have an existing Amazon account, you can use it to sign up with KDP. If you don't have an account, you should create one. It will only take a few minutes of your time.

5. Make sure that your internet browser is updated. Sometimes, if your browser is out of date, you can't access some of the features and functionality within the Kindle Publishing platform.

6. After completing the sign-up process, go the section that says Bookshelf, click on the button that says "Create a New Title", then click on the "Kindle eBook" option.

7. In the new window, you will be required to input your information and details about your book. These include Kindle eBook Details, Kindle eBook Content, and Kindle eBook Pricing.

8. After completing the steps above, just click "Publish Your Kindle eBook" and you're done. Your book will now go through the Amazon review process, which can take as long as 48 hours or less.

9. Voila! Your book is now published and ready to be read by people from all over the world.

Amazon Kindle Direct Publishing is a great source of passive income for the simple reason that once you published the book, there's very little work you have to do. You can focus most of your time on promoting and marketing the book. That in itself is a breeze if you have a marketing plan in place. In fact, you can also automate the marketing campaign so that you don't have to devote a lot of time on it. Some writers hire freelance content marketers and social media marketers to do the marketing for them.

Ratings Based on Our Criteria

A. **Simplicity:**
As long as your manuscript is up to par with Amazon's standards, there's very little barriers along the way. You can have your book published by Amazon in a few days.
9/10

B. **Passivity:**
Most of the hard work in Kindle publishing is over once you have finished your book. After submitting and publishing your book, the majority of the proceeds are passive in nature.
8/10

C. **Scalability:**
To scale your publishing business you can either write more books or create bundles using your existing books. The more books you have the more royalties you can earn from sales. If you intend on earning significantly more, you may want to consider promoting your books via your blog, to your email list or simply taking advantage of the Amazon marketing service (AMS). Finally, it'll be wise to have paperback and audio versions of your book in order to increase your chance of making a sale.
8/10

D. **Competitiveness:**
You have to understand that the book business is one of the most competitive fields out there. To put things into perspective, Amazon alone publishes dozens of books every single day. To minimize competition, you'll have to do a number of things right e.g. effective niche/keyword research (find profitable niches with great demand but little competition), great cover design for your book, compelling book description, book metadata optimized for relevant keywords etc.
2/10

Tips for Success

- Do your research. There are a lot of questions that you need answers to before you sit down and write your book. What niches and topics are the most profitable? Do non-fiction books sell more than fiction books? How much should you price your book? These are just some of the important questions you need to research on.

- Hire a professional book cover designer to create the cover for your book. A lot of the people browsing through Amazon's book section judge books by their covers. Everyone is guilty of this habit whether you like it or not. We often buy books for the simple reason that we liked the cover. In the same light, we don't buy books because of how ugly the covers are. So set aside a little bit of your budget to hire a good cover designer.

- Offer a few chapters of your book for free. This is a very common strategy for first-time authors. If you are confident about the quality of your content, then you shouldn't worry too much about providing some chapters for free. This strategy allows potential readers to get a taste of what you're offering.

- Send out free copies of your book to reviewers and bloggers in your niche. This is a great way to start your word-of-mouth marketing. Bloggers and digital influencers love getting free stuff and if they enjoyed your book, there's the likelihood that they'll write a glowing review about it. However, never ask for a review in exchange for giving out free copies. This is against Amazons terms and conditions.

- Create a blog around your book. There will be readers of your book who will like your book enough to want to learn more about you, what you do, or maybe other content you wrote that's related to the topics in the book. You can fulfill this need by writing a blog.

- Create a Facebook page for your book. This is free and easy to do so there's absolutely no reason why you shouldn't do it. Treat your Facebook page as a portal where you get to connect with those who have read your book and those who might be interested in reading it.

- Think about writing a series. Many of modern publishing's most successful writers made a name for themselves by writing book series. Just think of JK Rowling, Robert Ludlum, Clive Cussler, etc. These are authors who wrote numerous books featuring the same characters. It's a powerful strategy. You should try it and see where it goes.

- Collaborate with other writers. As much as possible, you should only work with writers who are your equals or your betters. Always remember that you are collaborating with them so that you can use their clout and influence as leverage to promote your book.

- Advertise your book. To make money, you have to spend money. A good place to start advertising your book is Google Adsense. Make sure to use relevant keywords in your ads so that the ads will appear in websites and blogs that are relevant to your book's content.

- Run contests and giveaways. You can run these contests and giveaways on a variety of platforms (i.e. blog, website, Facebook page, Twitter, Instagram, etc.). You can also leverage book promotion sites to help bring exposure to your book. If you want 127 of the top free and paid book promotion sites you can use for this purpose, go to *www.Kindlepreneur.com/list-sites-promote-free-amazon-books*

Frequently Asked Questions and Answers

- Is it free to publish a book on Amazon Kindle?
    - Yes, publishing your book through Amazon Direct Kindle Publishing is absolutely free. This applies to both ebook and paperback versions of your book. You don't have to pay a penny to get your book published.

- How long does it take for the book to be published and become available for sale?
    - After uploading your manuscript and all the necessary sections of the book, it usually takes between 24 and 48 hours for your book to officially appear on Amazon's listings.

- What is the process in publishing a book on Amazon?
    - The process is quite simple. One, create an Amazon account. Two, log into Amazon Kindle Publishing. Three, add your address, personal information, bank information, and tax information. Four, upload the final manuscript for your book. And five, hit the publish button.

- What do I do if I encounter a problem during the publication of my book?

- The first thing you should do is contact Amazon support immediately. There's a specific customer support for writers using Amazon Direct Kindle Publishing so you should approach them first. You should also consider seeking help from other authors through Amazon's Author Central page. Those authors who have encountered the same problem as yours may be able to help you out.

- How much should I price a book I publish on Amazon?
  - It's up to you. There's no floor or ceiling on how much you want customers to pay for your book. You can price it at 99 cents or $10.

- How much money can I earn from my book?
  - It depends on several factors. Is it your first book? Do you already have an established following? How good is your book? What niche does it belong to? How much budget do you have for your marketing campaign? These are just some of the factors that will ultimately determine how much you are going to earn from your book.

- How many books can I publish on Amazon Kindle?
  - You can publish as many books as you like as long as these adhere to Kindle's rules and standards.

- How do I promote my book on Amazon Kindle?
  - There are a lot of ways. These include blogging, social media marketing, advertising, running contests, and giving away copies of your book to reviewers and digital influencers.

- Will Amazon ever remove my book from its listings?
  - Yes, that is definitely a possibility. But you have nothing to worry about if your book hasn't broken any of the platform's rules and regulations.

- Will my book be available to anyone from around the world?
  - Yes, if you choose to. As the author, you have the option to decide whether your book is going to be available worldwide or on a select locations/countries only.

Myth Busters About Kindle Direct Publishing

- Self-publishing ebooks on Kindle is easy and instantly profitable. No, it's not. A huge percentage of self-publishers on Amazon make very little from their work. You need to do things the right way to succeed i.e. effective niche/keyword research (profitable niches with great demand and little competition), good cover design, compelling book description, metadata optimized for keywords etc.

- You need an original idea. Not necessarily. You can use the works of others as inspiration (That being said, do not copy other people's work. This can potentially get your KDP account suspended).

- You need a big launch party to sell your book. If your book is good enough and if you market it enough, people will come to you.

- There are too many ebooks already. Yes, indeed, but that doesn't mean you can't add your own book to the pool. Infact, with effective niche research, you can minimize competition and still make a healthy profit!

- You need an agent. Nope, there's a reason why it's called self-publishing. You do it without an agent.

- Amazon will own your ebook if you publish it on Kindle. Not true. You still have all the rights to your book. You're only using Amazon as your selling platform.

- You need at least 20 reviews to appear in Amazon's "Also Bought" feature. Not true. Books with less than 20 reviews also appear on "Also Bought" lists.

- The more reviews your book gets, the higher it will appear in Amazon's search results. Not true. Doing a quick search on the site can easily disprove this. Furthermore, other factors like sales, relevance and keyword optimization (in the title, subtitle, book description etc.) affect how well your book will rank.

- Reviews affect your book's sales rank. It has some effect but it's not substantial. The biggest factors in determining sales rank are purchased and number of downloads.

- Kindle Select's 90-day exclusivity also applies to paperback versions of your book. Not true. The 90-day exclusivity only applies to ebooks.

Congratulations!

The second character of the password required to unlock the business scorecard is letter i.

Inspiration #2

"Opportunities don't happen. You create them"

Chris Grosser

Business #2

Amazon FBA (Fulfilled by Amazon)

Fulfilled by Amazon or FBA is an e-commerce program by the online retail giant. The program's business model is very similar to that of dropshipping. If you are familiar with dropshipping or if you have experience with it, you will find it easy to understand Amazon FBA's business model. This opportunity can be very lucrative if you can think of a product that has very little competition within the Amazon network. The whole process can be simplified in the following steps:

1. You apply for the Amazon FBA program.
2. If you are accepted, you ship your products to one of their distribution centers. The company refers to these distribution centers as fulfilment centers.
3. You list your products for sale in Amazon.
4. If someone buys your product, Amazon ships the product to the customer.

Looking at the business model of the program, it's easy to recognize obvious benefits. For one, Amazon handles the sales and shipping process. The company receives the orders, process them, and ship the products. They are literally running the business for you. Your main responsibility is to keep on sending more of your products to Amazon's fulfilment centers before these run out of stock.

Earlier, we've mentioned how the business model is very similar to dropshipping. This is because you can turn it into a real dropshipping business. You can enter into a contract with a manufacturer or a supplier who makes the products then ship these on your behalf to Amazon's fulfilment centers. In this setup, your role is to make sure that the supplier keeps making and shipping the products. You can also choose to have the supplier send the products to you so that you will be the one shipping the products to Amazon. This is a good idea if you want to make sure that the products you are selling are of the highest quality possible.

Ratings Based on Our Criteria

A. **Simplicity:**
   Starting a business with Amazon FBA can be very complicated because there are a lot of hoops you have to go through. You have to apply with the program. You need to make sure that the products pass certain standards (e.g. packaging and safety requirements) etc. And you have to be communicating with your manufacturer/supplier, inspectors etc. to make sure products are manufactured to specification. If they happen to be in China, the language barrier and time zone difference could present challenges.

   6/10

B. **Passivity:**
   Managing an Amazon FBA business can take a lot of your time and resources. Some of your time will be spent communicating with your suppliers, optimizing your listings, running promotions/giveaways, Optimizing your Amazon sponsored ads etc. However, passivity can be improved by outsourcing some of these tasks to virtual assistants who will take care of them for you. Virtual assistants can be hired from fiverr.com or upwork.com.

   6/10

C. **Scalability:**
   It's easy to scale your Amazon FBA business. Once you are accepted into the program and you have successfully launched your first product and familiarized yourself with the process, scaling is as simple as adding more products to your inventory or expanding your product offerings (i.e. offering your customers complementary products as part of a bundle).

9/10

D. **Competitiveness:**
Expect a lot of other merchants selling similar products as you. You might even be getting your products from the same suppliers. Furthermore, it's not unusual to compete directly with suppliers from China.

4/10

Tips For Success

- Do your research before you jump into the bandwagon. As I've mentioned earlier, competition within Amazon is fierce. So what you need to do is research for products that have good demand but little competition. A good market research software for this is Jungle Scout or Viral Launch

- Watch and observe your most successful competitors. What are they doing? What tools are they using? What marketing strategies are they implementing? Learn about these and maybe apply them on your own business.

- Encourage your customers to leave reviews. The more reviews you get on Amazon, the greater the social proof and likelihood of it selling. However, do not offer incentives in exchange for review as this is against Amazon's terms of service.

- Optimize your product listings with the right keywords and descriptions. A good keyword research tool to consider is Merchant Words

- Use high-quality photos of your products. Ugly and unprofessional product photos can easily turn off customers.

- Only deal with reliable manufacturers and suppliers. If they screw up, then your business is equally screwed.

- Always check with Amazon to ensure that your products are in stock. Running out of stock can negatively affect your product rankings and once lost its difficult to regain.

- Personalize/brand your products to make them stand out from the others. This is important if you are getting your products from a supplier who is probably sending the same products to other merchants.

- Offer discounts and incentives to those who are buying in bulk. This is a great way to build loyalty among your customers.

- Always follow the rules, regulations, and standards as set forth by Amazon. Amazon can easily terminate your account if you break a rule or two.

Frequently Asked Questions and Answers

- What are the requirements in joining Amazon FBA?
  - You are going to need the following: email address, standard mailing address, phone number, social security number, tax identification number, credit or debit card, bank account, and bank routing number.

- What are the costs of using Amazon FBA?

- When using FBA, you should expect to be paying for three specific types of fees: storage fees, fulfilment fees, and inventory placement fees. These are not fixed fees. They depend on the types of products you are sending them for storage. They will inform you about the amount of fees you are going to pay after finalizing your shipments.

- How do I get products ready for Amazon FBA?
  - Every product you have must be individually packaged, properly labelled, and ready to be sold. You should also strictly follow the company's product stickering requirements.

- Can I sell products overseas through Amazon FBA?
  - Yes, you absolutely can. Amazon is flexible when it comes to importing or exporting your products. However, you should keep in mind that selling your products overseas has additional fees, requirements, and other complications. Make sure that you take this into account and look into your financials to see if it's worth it to offer your products to overseas customers.

- How do I ship my products to any of Amazon's fulfilment centers?
  - The full procedure is detailed in Amazon FBA's help section. You have to log into your Amazon FBA account, go to Manage Inventory and choose the Send and Replenish Inventory option. You have to completely and properly label your products before you ship them to Amazon's fulfilment centers. Improperly packaged products will cause a lot of problems which can be very costly on your part.

- What kind of products can I sell through Amazon FBA?
  - Amazon FBA has a long list of restricted products so I highly suggest that you check it out. Here's the list of products that you can't sell on Amazon FBA as an independent seller:
    - Alcohol
    - Warranties, service plans, contracts and guarantees
    - Tobacco and tobacco-related products
    - Throwable personal flotation devices
    - Surveillance equipment
    - Subscriptions and periodicals
    - String lights
    - Stolen property and lock picking devices
    - Squishy toys
    - Sex and sensuality products
    - Recycled electronics
    - Recalled products
    - FBA prohibited products exceptions
    - Postage meters and stamps
    - Plants, seeds, and other plant products
    - Pesticides
    - Personal electronic mobility devices or PEMs
    - Organic products
    - Offensive and controversial materials
    - Medical devices and accessories
    - Lighting products
    - Laser products
    - Jewelry and precious gems
    - Invisible ink pens
    - Infant sleep positioners

- Infant car seats
- Human parts and burial artefacts
- Hazardous and dangerous items
- Gambling and lottery products
- Chilled and frozen foods
- Food and beverages
- Fire and smoke masks
- Fire and other safety products
- Fidget spinners
- Export controls
- Explosives, weapons, and related items
- Electronics
- Eclipse glasses and filters for solar viewing
- Drugs and drug paraphernalia
- Dietary supplements
- Currency, coins, cash equivalents, and gift cards
- Cosmetics and skin and hair care
- Batteries and chargers
- Automotive and powersports
- Art home décor
- Fine art
- Animals and animal products
- Amazon devices: Fair Use and Compatibility Guidelines
- Amazon Device Accessories

- How safe are my products when I ship them to Amazon?
  - There is always the possibility that your products can get lost during transit and storage. However, these problems are rare. As to security, Amazon has a payment fraud protection system that protects you from fraudulent orders and transactions.

- How much does it cost to sell on Amazon?
  - Amazon offers two types of plans. The Professional Selling Plan costs $39.99 a month plus per item selling fees. The Individual Selling Plan is for sellers who only sells 40 items or less a month. This plan doesn't have a monthly fee. Instead, you pay a $0.99 fee for every item you sell.

- Who handles customer support on my Amazon FBA products?
  - Customer support is the responsibility of Amazon. This is one of the biggest advantages of the Amazon FBA program. Once you shipped your products to their fulfilment centers, the company will handle the rest. They will manage customer inquiries, refunds, and returns. It's worth mentioning here that Amazon's customer support is available 24 hours a day, seven days a week.

- Where can I get products to sell on Amazon FBA?
  - There are several avenues that you can explore here. One, you can create your own products. Two, you can enter a deal with a supplier who provides you with products which you then label and package as your own. Three, you can explore retail arbitrage. That is you purchase products from other stores in bulk then sell them for a profit on Amazon. And four, you can consider private labelling or white labelling.

Myth Busters About Amazon FBA

- That it's very hard to sell products on Amazon. Yes, the system seems complicated but it's actually easy once you get the hang of it.

- That you can't be successful selling on Amazon because of the immense competition. Sure, the competition is tough but the market is also growing. In short, Amazon is still a very profitable side business.

- That you can just list your product and it will start selling like hotcakes. If you are to achieve success on Amazon, you don't just list a product, you have to market it like crazy.

- That you need your own website to sell on Amazon. Amazon itself serves as your online store. List your product and the company does the rest.

- That you need to invest a lot of money into Amazon. You can start a business on Amazon with just a few hundred dollars. In short, it's not that expensive.

- That inventory management is a pain in the head. Yes, it can be confusing at first but just like everything else, you will get used to it.

- That you need to give a lot of discounts to attract customers. Offering discounts surely helps but you don't have to if you are confident about the demand for your products.

- That Amazon doesn't care about you. The fact that the company welcomes independent sellers tells a very different story.

- That Amazon is losing its influence. This myth is perpetrated by competitors who want to steal sellers from Amazon and bring them into their own platforms.

- That you can get rich quick on Amazon. Don't entertain such an exaggerated idea. Of course, it's possible but you should be realistic with your goals.

Inspiration #3

"There are two types of people who will tell you that you cannot make a difference in this world: those who are afraid to try and those who are afraid you will succeed."

Ray Goforth

Business #3

Blogging

The basics of earning money from a blog are quite simple. You create a blog, publish valuable content in it, then monetize it using any of various monetization methods like affiliate marketing, direct advertising, third-party advertising, etc. If you write the content yourself, the income you earn can still be considered as partly passive. But if you want to truly turn a blog into a source of real passive income, what you should do is outsource the content-creation process to freelance writers. You are going to pay other people to write the content that you are going to publish in your blog. With that said, you are not the one actively performing the difficult work of creating content.

Finding freelance content creators is not that hard. There are dozens of job sites and classified ads sites out there where you can find good writers offering affordable rates. These sites include Upwork, Fiverr, Freelancer, Craigslist, and even LinkedIn. What you do is hire a qualified writer then send him a list of keywords that will be the topics of his articles. It's as simple as that. Have the articles written, hone them to perfection, and then publish them on your blog. Then rinse and repeat. The more quality content you put in your blog, the more visitors it will attract. More traffic means more passive income (only if the affiliate products you promote on your blog are relevant to your visitors)

Ratings Based on Our Criteria

A. **Simplicity:**
Starting a blog is rather easy. In fact you can create one in just a few minutes.
9/10

B. **Passivity:**
Even if you outsource most of your content-creation process, the earnings you make won't be 100% passive. You still have to perform tasks like reading and replying to comments, brainstorming for new ideas, and communicating with advertisers and partners.
7/10

C. **Scalability:**
Blogging is highly scalable in the sense that you can duplicate your success in a specific niche by applying the same tactics in another niche. In addition, the same blog that serves 100 people can also serve 100,000 people without any significant increase in your fixed costs. If you're interested in learning how to set up a six figure blog/website, this article on my website will help you.
7/10

D. **Competitiveness:**
The blogging sphere is very competitive in the sense that there are literally millions of blogs out there on just about every subject. Simplicity can be a double-edged sword because the easier the business opportunity, the lower the barrier to entry.
2/10

Tips for Success

- Focus your attention on a specific niche. It's much easier to attract a following online if you keep on writing articles that revolve around a specific topic. It encourages people to return to your blog because they know the type of content you publish.

- Focus on quality, not quantity. One good article will earn you more money than ten bad articles.

- Optimize your articles for search engines. This is a no-brainer when it comes to blogging and content marketing. If you want people to find your blog posts, you should optimize them with the right keywords.

- Promote your blog on social media. For example, you should create a Twitter, Instagram and Facebook page that links directly to your blog.

- Enable comments in your blog posts. Readers who want to say something should be allowed to chime in. This encourages interaction.

- Make your blog as simple as possible. Readers hate cluttered websites. You should get rid of unnecessary widgets, buttons, etc.

- Follow a posting schedule. This is very important if you want to build a legion of followers. Nothing turns off a reader more than a stagnant blog. You can follow a daily posting schedule, a three times a week posting schedule, or a weekly schedule. What's important is that you stick to it so that readers will know when to expect new content from you.

- Turn reader comments into content. This is why it's good to turn on the comments in every blog post you make. Feedback by readers is a great source for ideas for upcoming posts.

- Use images, videos, and infographics in your blog posts. Articles can become boring at times so make it a point to spice things up by adding other types of media into your content.

- Make it easy for readers to share your blog posts. At the end of every article you post, there should be buttons there that allow readers to share the article on social media or through email. You can attract a lot of new readers from this strategy alone.

Frequently Asked Questions and Answers

- How do I start a blog?
  - You have two options. If you have web development skills, you can build one from scratch. If not, you can start with a blogging platform like Wordpress and Blogger.

- How much do I need to spend to create and build a blog?
  - It depends. Your main expenses would be composed of the amounts you pay for domain registration and hosting.

- How often do I need to update my blog?
  - It depends on your target audience and your topic. If you are talking about current news and events, you probably need to update the blog every day.

- How do I monetize a blog?
  - There are several monetization methods that you can explore. These include direct advertising, affiliate marketing (Amazon, ClickBank, and eBay), sponsored posts, and advertising programs (Adsense).

- I'm not very tech-savvy. Can I still make money from a blog?

- Of course, you can. There are a lot of simple tools and resources that you can use to start a blog even if you can't write a single line of code.

- How do I drive traffic to my blog?
  - There are so many ways. These include social media marketing, search engine optimization, advertising, and content marketing.

- What is a niche?
  - A niche is a specific topic or theme which becomes the focus of your blog. If your blog is about basketball news and updates, then you are in the "basketball niche".

- Can I really make money from blogging?
  - Yes. Hundreds of thousands of bloggers are currently doing it. If they can, then you can as well.

- Should I get my own domain name for my blog?
  - Although it's possible to make money from a free-hosted blog on Blogger or Wordpress, it's highly recommended that you register your own domain name. It makes you look more professional and readers are more likely to take you serious.

- Should I learn search engine optimization?
  - Yes, it's absolutely necessary that you learn at least the basics of search engine optimization (SEO) and apply these on your blog. It's one of the most effective ways on how to attract more people to your blog. Alternatively, you can partner with someone who is very tech savvy.

Myth Busters About Blogging

- If you build it, they will come. Nope, they won't. Building a blog is just one aspect of blogging. With thousands of blogs being created and published every single day, yours can easily be lost in the immense stream. So don't just build it, you should also market and promote it like your life depends on it.

- You can easily make money blogging. Nope, you can't and you won't unless you are Stephen King or JK Rowling. Earning money from a blog requires hard work and patience. For most bloggers, it can take months or even years before you get a significant amount of income coming your way.

- Blogging is just a fad. If blogging is just a fad, then it should be dead in the water by now. Blogging started gaining traction more than a decade ago but it's still going strong. In fact, more and more people are starting blogs these days given the ease of building one.

- If you can't write well, you can't have your own blog. Newsflash, freelance content creators exist. If you can't write, you can always hire an army of freelance writers to do the dirty work for you.

- You have to post everyday if you want readers to keep coming back to your blog. No, you don't. In fact, posting everyday can overwhelm your readers.

- You need to be tech-savvy and have coding skills to start blogging. Quite the contrary because anyone who knows how to click a mouse can start a blog.

- There's not much to learn about blogging. If you tell yourself this, then you are setting yourself up for failure. The blogging space is evolving. There are new things to learn every single day.

- Free themes are just as good as paid themes. In a certain way this is true but if you are serious about blogging, you really need to get a paid theme that is uniquely yours.
- You need comments on your blog to be successful. Not true. Some of the most popular blogs out there have their comments section turned off.
- Social media is useless for blogging. You are missing out on a lot of opportunities if you don't link your blog to your different social media platforms.

Inspiration #4

"Successful people do what unsuccessful people are not willing to do. Don't wish it were easier; wish you were better."

Jim Rohn

Business #4

Domain Flipping

There are three main categories of domain flipping. One, you build a website from scratch then offer it for sale with a healthy profit margin. Two, you purchase an already built website, put a mark-up on your purchasing price, then resell it without changing the website. And three, you buy a website, improve upon it, then sell it for profit. Domain flipping is basically the business of purchasing and selling websites. This can be a very lucrative source of passive income if you know how to spot premium domains that you can sell at huge profits. It's about creating websites and improving websites with the sole intention of selling them for profit.

Needless to say, to be successful in this arena, you should have knowledge and skills in web development, coding, and programming. You should be able to build professional-looking websites at great speed.

To look for the people who might be interested in buying websites you created, you should sign up with the top domain flipping websites. These are websites that were built specifically for buyers and sellers of domains and websites e.g. www.Flippa.com. Some of these domain flipping websites charge membership fees but most of them are free to use. So there's absolutely no reason why you shouldn't utilize them to your advantage. Just sign up, customize your profile, and then list the domains you are selling. In some instances, the domain flipping website will take a percentage cut from your sales. It's important that you take into account these percentage cuts when pricing your domains for sale.

To be successful in the domain flipping business, you have to be a trend watcher. What does this mean? It means you should be on the lookout for the hottest trends and developments in the web. For instance, there's a new dance craze called "ABC Dancing" that's taking the internet by storm. If you are a trend watcher, you will be among those who will first be aware of this new dance trend. Putting your domain flipper hat on, you then start registering domain names that might be in demand in the next day, weeks, or months. Such domain names can be abcdancing.com, abcdancing.net, abcdancinglessons.com, etc. In a nutshell, you have to be a forward thinker.

You should learn how to spot these trends then cash in on them before anyone else can. A good tool to help with researching trends is Google Trends

Ratings Based on Our Criteria

A. Simplicity:

Domain flipping is quite simple in the sense that there's very little work associated with it especially if you focus on purchasing and selling the domains. Of course it's a little bit more complicated if you build the websites yourself from scratch.

8/10

B. Passivity:

Building websites from scratch, buying and improving websites, and promoting websites for sale can take a lot of your time and resources. To improve passivity, you may want to document the process of trend research and domain purchase. You can then hire a virtual assistant who will handle these tasks for you. Alternatively, you can just outsource the research and promotion tasks and focus only on the buying and selling.

6/10

C. Scalability:

Domain flipping is one of the most scalable business models online. You can pretty much scale the business overnight as long as you have the funds to purchase sites. The more valuable digital assets you have (i.e. sites), the more you can potentially earn.

9/10

D. Competitiveness:

There are thousands of other domain flippers out there. It also happens that there are only a few marketplaces for websites that are up for sale. In short, the competition can be tough.

4/10

Tips for Success

- Do not be afraid to take risks. Flipping domains is kind of a gamble. You should be more than willing to gamble with domains that you think are going to be profitable. For example, let's say you come across a domain for sale that looks promising but has a steep price. If your experience tells you that the domain might be profitable down the line, then go and purchase it.

- Choose a niche that you are familiar with. If you are knowledgeable about the niche, then you know what kinds of terms and phrases are popular within the niche. Register these words and phrases as domains and sooner or later someone will be calling to buy the domains from you.

- Visit domain auction sites and see what kinds of domains are in demand. For example, you can check out GoDaddy Auction and get an idea of the kinds of domains that are getting the highest prices.

- Be mindful of the domain extensions that you are using. Pay attention to the three most common extensions (.com, .net, and, .org). For example, if the domain successfulbusiness.com is not available, maybe the domains successfulbusiness.net and successfulbusiness.org are still unregistered. You have to be creative in brainstorming for domain ideas.

- Be on the lookout for expired domain names. These are websites that expired and remains unrenewed by their original registrants. These expired domains are valuable in the sense that they already have page ranks and backlinks.

- Create high-quality content for a domain before you offer it for sale. Good content can double or even triple the value and asking price of a domain. If you are selling numerous domains, try hiring a freelance writer to create the content for them.

- Stay up to date with regards to latest news, trends, and developments in your niche. Maybe there's a new word or phrase that becomes very popular in your niche. You can quickly register the word or phrase as a domain name. Again, this is a bit of a gamble but it can prove very profitable if the domain you registered eventually comes in demand.

- Always be on the lookout for discounts and offers from the biggest domain registration companies like GoDaddy. You can save a lot of money this way. If a company offers a promo period where domains are available for $1 each, jump in and get as many promising domains as you can. Just imagine the profit you can make if you are able to sell the domains for $100 and up.

- Create an account in the top domain registrars. The biggest domain registrars today are Namecheap, Bluehost, HostGator, GoDaddy, and Dreamhost. It would be a good idea to create an account with all of them so you can take advantage of their promos, discounts, coupons, and other offers. Creating an account with them is free so you have nothing to lose.

- Treat your domain flipping efforts as a business. This means you should create a website which will serve as your business headquarters. This is where people can look at all the domains you have for sale.

Frequently Asked Questions and Answers

- How does domain flipping work and how do I make money from it?
  - Domain flipping follows the buy and sell model. You buy websites then sell them for a profit. Or you can create websites from scratch then sell them to interested buyers.

- Where can I buy and sell domains?
  - There are several domain flipping platforms that you can use. These include Flippa, Sedo, Afternic, Igloo, Cax, BrandBucket, HuntingMoon, SnapNames, Pool, GoDaddy Premium Listings, Bido, Undeveloped, and even eBay.

- How do I start flipping domains?
  - First of all, make sure that you have everything you need to get started. You should sign up with an online marketplace like Flippa where you can buy and sell domains. After signing up, you are free to list the domains you want to sell as well as purchase the domains you are interested in acquiring.

- Is domain flipping still profitable?
  - Yes, of course it's still profitable. There are thousands of individuals and businesses out there looking for a good domain name every single day. To be successful in domain flipping, you should have an eye for the latest trends and where they're going. For example, a new dance craze hits the dance scene. If you are smart, you should immediately starting registering domains and building websites around the words and phrases that describe the craze.

- How much should I price a domain I'm selling?
  - There are several factors that you need to consider when pricing a domain. How much did you pay for it? How much did you spend in building it if you created it yourself? Do you think the domain's value accrue over time? Is it just a domain or you've published lots of content on it? These are just some of the considerations you must take into account when putting a price tag on a domain.

- How do I market and promote the domains I'm selling?
  - There are several marketing strategies that you can use like search engine optimization, social media marketing, and advertising.

- How do I increase the value of the domains I'm selling?
  - You can significantly increase the asking price for a domain by simply creating content for it. Focus on a niche to build a steady flow of traffic towards the website. A steady traffic can double or even triple the value of the website.

- Where and how do I buy a website that I can then offer for sale?
  - You can purchase websites from any domain flipping website like Flippa, Igloo, and Sedo.

- I'm not a web developer. Can I still be a successful domain flipper?

- Yes, you can. Web development is a skill you only need if you are going to build websites from scratch or if you improve the websites you buy. But if you are going to simply purchase and sell websites, you don't need to be a web developer or programmer.

- How long should I hold on to an expired domain?
  - It depends on the influence and metrics of the domain. If it's a fairly good domain with decent traffic, you should probably sell it as soon as possible before it loses some of its value.

Myth Busters About Domain Flipping

- There aren't any affordable .com domains out there. Not true. If you look hard enough, you will find premium .com domains with affordable price tags.

- GoDaddy is the greatest domain registration company today. For sure, it is the most popular but that doesn't mean there aren't competitive alternatives. There are other companies like Namecheap who offer similar, if not better services.

- All the profitable domains have already been taken. This is just not true on many levels. If you are creative enough, you can research and find good and profitable domains that are yet to be registered.

- Registering numerous domain names at a time is unethical. Some web developers look at domain flippers as selfish and greedy entrepreneurs. No, they are not. It's just business. There's a market for domains so they are in the business of buying and selling them.

- Domains with .com extensions rank higher than domains with less common extensions (i.e. co, org, net). The domain extension does play a role in a website's search rankings but it's only applicable in rare instances. The quality of the website's content still remains as the most important factor in determining a website's worth and search rankings.

- You can master domain flipping in a few weeks' time. Domain flipping is not just about buying and selling domains and websites. You must have the background as well as the experience to spot what domains are profitable. This takes time to learn and master.
- Domain flipping is easy money. Nothing is farther from the truth. Just to provide you some hard truth, majority of domain flippers don't make that much money from the business. Only a few domain flippers earn full-time from their efforts. This is not an attempt to discourage you. We just want you to be realistic about how much you are going to earn if you start flipping domains and websites.

- Build the websites and domain buyers will start coming. Yes, there's some truth to this if you can build beautiful and great websites. However, the adage that if you build them, customers will start coming isn't exactly true. You still have to do a lot of marketing and promotion to attract potential domain buyers.

- Domain flipping is not susceptible to fraud and hacking. This is not true. Just like any online business model, domain flipping has its own problems with regards to fraud and hacking. Hackers can hack into your accounts in domain flipping websites and steal the sites you've registered and created.

- Inevitably, social profiles are bound to replace the domain names. A lot of people in the marketing and advertising industry are worried that the growing popularity of social media networks will force businesses to focus on their social media presence and stop building their own sites. This isn't happening at all.

Inspiration #5

"Success is walking from failure to failure with no loss of enthusiasm."
Winston S. Churchill

Series #	Book Title
1	Affiliate Marketing
2	Passive Income Ideas
3	Affiliate Marketing + Passive Income Ideas (2-in-1 Bundle)
4	Facebook Advertising
5	Dropshipping
6	Dropshipping + Facebook Advertising (2-in-1 Bundle)
7	Real Estate Investing For Beginners
8	Credit Cards and Credit Repair Secrets
9	Real Estate Investing And Credit Repair Strategies (2-in-1 Bundle)
10	Passive Income Ideas With Affiliate Marketing (2nd Edition)
11	Passive Income With Dividend Investing
12	Stock Market Investing For Beginners
13	The Simple Stock Market Investing Blueprint (2-in-1 Bundle)
14	Real Estate And Stock Market Investing Mastery (3-in-1 Bundle)
15	Amazon FBA Mastery

Download The Audio Versions Along With The Complementary PDF Document For FREE from www.MichaelEzeanaka.com

Business #5

Shopify

If you want to build your own e-commerce store, Shopify is a platform you should seriously consider using. There's a reason why this platform is one of the biggest players in online commerce today. Hundreds of thousands of entrepreneurs and merchants use the platform to market and sell their products. Shopify is great for two things. It's great for starting an e-commerce store. And it's great for building a dropshipping business. The company offers several plans for those interested in using their services. These plans and their corresponding rates (as of July 2018) are as follows:

- Basic Shopify: $29 per month
- Standard Shopify: $79 per month
- Advanced Shopify: $299 per month
- Shopify Lite: $9 per month
- Shopify Plus: Flexible rate per month

If you are still not sure if Shopify is the appropriate platform for you, you can always test their free trial version. This trial version allows you access to Shopify's most basic features and functions for free for a period of fourteen (14) days. There are no strings attached. You can cancel and terminate your account any time you want. If you want to continue with the service, you will be given time to choose from the various plans (i.e. Basic Shopify, Standard Shopify, Shopify Lite, Advanced Shopify, and Shopify Plus).

Using Shopify to build an online business is quite easy and hassle-free. This is one of the most important selling points of the platform. It allows you to create a professional-looking e-commerce store even if you have very limited knowledge about web development, coding, and programming in general. The platform has a website builder wherein all you have to do is choose the template and customize it using pre-fabricated options, features, and functions. There are dozens of templates that you can use for free. Another great thing about these templates is that they have been designed specifically for certain niches and markets. For example, there are templates that have been designed for online stores selling shirts and other apparel.

If you don't have your own products to sell, no problem. You can always choose the dropshipping route. What you do is create your Shopify store and list products that you will be ordering from a manufacturer or supplier. You will not be keeping any product inventory. In fact, you won't even be the one shipping the products to your customers. If a customer orders a product from your Shopify store, your store orders the product from your supplier. The supplier then ships the product to your customer. Although the product came from your supplier, it looks like it came from you. This process can be 100% automated which means you earn money around the clock. It's nearly 100% passive income. You don't make the products and you are not the one shipping them. The cost of running the business is really cheap. Your major expenses will only be composed of your monthly dues from Shopify and any amount you spend on advertising and other marketing campaigns.

Ratings Based on Our Criteria

A. **Simplicity:**
   The greatest thing about Shopify is that anyone can use the platform to build professional-looking online stores. Even if you have zero coding or programming skills, creating a store using their website builder is a breeze.

   9/10

B. **Passivity:**

Your store can be fully automated especially if you are following the dropshipping model. Additionally, there are tons of apps that you can use to make it easier to run and manage the business.

8/10

C. **Scalability:**

There's no limit to the number of Shopify stores that you can make. As long as you follow the rules and terms of agreement, there's no limit to how big you can grow your store. Of course, there's also the fact that you can list thousands of products in a single Shopify store.

9/10

D. **Competitiveness:**

There's a lot of competition within the Shopify platform, that's for sure. But if you are confident about the quality of your products and the speed at which you deliver them, then you have very little to be worried about.

4/10

Tips For Success

- Take advantage of the platform's free trial version to familiarize yourself with the features and functions. The trial version will run for a period of fourteen (14) days.
- Customize your online store for branding reasons. Make it unique so that it will stand out from the competition. Never forget the possibility that there are other merchants on the platform selling the same products as you. If they have better websites than you, then customers will likely choose them over you.
- Focus on product quality, not quantity. Many new merchants on Shopify often make the mistake of assuming that the more products they list on their e-commerce website, the more sales they can make. This is a terrible approach in building a business. Quality should always be your main focus.
- Promote your Shopify store whenever and wherever you can. Don't solely rely on the platform to send you customers. You should exert efforts in driving high-quality and targeted traffic to your website.
- Make sure that your store is supported on a wide variety of devices such as desktops, laptops, mobile phones, and tablets.
- Make it as easy as possible for a customer to navigate through your website. Customers should be able to see how much a product costs with just a click or a tap.
- Always perform analytics to see what's working and what's not working. Shopify has its own analytics program but if you are not satisfied with it, you can also use Google Analytics.
- Set up a blog for your store. Your Shopify store normally comes with a built-in blog but this won't be enough. You should try building a separate blog in another domain and use it to drive organic traffic to your store.
- Run giveaways. This is a great way to engage your existing customers and to raise awareness about your store and products.
- Build an email list. You have no idea how much repeat customers you can get by simply sending updates to your email list.

Frequently Asked Questions and Answers

- What is Shopify and how does it work?
  - It's an ecommerce platform and website builder that allows you to create your own online store.

- What products can you sell on Shopify?
  - You can sell both physical products and digital products or a combination of both.

- How much does Shopify cost?
  - Shopify collects a monthly fee from merchants and entrepreneurs depending on the type of plan they are on. Basic Shopify costs $29 a month. Standard Shopify costs $79 a month. And Advanced Shopify costs $299 a month. Other accounts like Shopify Lite and Shopify Plus cost $9 per month and $1000+ per month respectively.

- Does Shopify have a free trial version?
  - Yes, you can test their free trial version that runs for fourteen days.

- How many products can you sell on Shopify?
  - One of the biggest advantages of selling on Shopify is that there's no limit to the number of products you can list in your store.

- How do you collect payments from customers?
  - The company offers you several payment options.

- Can you collect payments via PayPal?
  - Yes, you can set up your store so that it can accept payments from PayPal and other companies that offer the same services.

- Can I build more than one stores on Shopify?
  - Many online entrepreneurs run several stores on the site so it's definitely possible.

- Does Shopify have a blogging feature?
  - Yes, Shopify has a blogging feature which enables you to write and create content to engage and attract customers.

- Can I use third-party apps on my Shopify store?
  - Yes. In fact, Shopify has its own app store where you can purchase apps for your online store. Many of the apps in the store are also free to use.

Myth Busters About Selling on Shopify

- That you can get rich quick on Shopify. Don't believe those self-proclaimed gurus that claim you can be a millionaire overnight with Shopify. It simply isn't true. Nothing worthwhile happens overnight. There's always a learning process.

- That Shopify is purely a dropshipping business. Yes, dropshipping is a large aspect of Shopify's business model but it's just half of what the company offers for entrepreneurs.

- That Shopify stores have a lot of security loopholes. This may be true several years ago but not today. The company is now one of the most secure ecommerce platforms in existence.

- That Shopify is very expensive. The company's most expensive plan costs only $299 a month. That's a bargain considering the tons of features and functions you get.

- That there's too much competition in Shopify. It's true that there's competition but it's the healthy kind of competition. If you have a good product and you market it well (i.e. emphasizing your unique value proposition etc.), you have very little to be worried about.

- That Shopify has poor customer support. Quite the contrary because Shopify happens to have one of the most efficient customer support system in the industry. They can be contacted via phone, email, and live chat.

- That Shopify stores are difficult to manage. Not true. When you log into Shopify, you can go to your admin panel and manage or even customize your store from there.

- That the number of products you can sell on the site are limited and controlled. The truth is Shopify allows you to upload as many product listings as you want.

- That Shopify is losing steam and will close operations in a few years' time. Shopify's stats and metrics are actually growing at a quick pace. Revenue is growing and the products being sold through the platform are getting better.

- That you need to be tech-savvy to build a store on Shopify. Shopify's website builder is simple enough to be understood by anyone who knows how to browse the internet.

Inspiration #6

"If you are not willing to risk the usual, you will have to settle for the ordinary."
Jim Rohn

Business #6

Freelancing as a Virtual Assistant

Hundreds of thousands of professionals from around the world make decent incomes as freelance virtual assistants. You can do the same if you have the determination to be successful in it. The job description for a virtual assistant is as varied as the number of virtual assistants out there. Think of yourself as someone's personal assistant or secretary but you perform your duties remotely and online. For example, a business owner can get you as a virtual assistant and your job is to read and reply to emails being sent to the business owner.

Or you can be a virtual assistant to a data analyst. Maybe you will be performing tasks like creating graphs or building presentations for sets of data. Or you can be a virtual assistant to a social media manager. Your tasks will include managing Facebook and Twitter pages for certain clients of the manager. The point here is that your tasks as a virtual assistant varies and depends on the specific industry that you're in. You can find virtual assistant job opportunities in websites like Odesk, Freelancer, and Craigslit.

As a virtual assistant, 100% of the tasks you perform are done remotely. You can work for months or even years for a boss without ever learning about what he or she looks like. There are no specific standard that govern what a virtual assistant does or doesn't do. As long as you are performing tasks remotely for a company or individual as an employee, then you can be considered as a virtual assistant. The term "virtual assistant" in itself defines what you do. You are an assistant but you work online.

Ratings Based on Our Criteria

A. **Simplicity:**
   I wouldn't describe the responsibilities of a virtual assistant as simple. There's no clear definition of what tasks you are supposed to do so sometimes you are at the mercy of your boss or employer.

   6/10

B. **Passivity:**
   Being a virtual assistant can't be really considered as a passive source of income since you are directly working for a fixed pay. It becomes passive if you hire a team of virtual assistants who will work under your wing. That way, you are not personally exchanging your time for money.

   5/10

C. **Scalability:**
   It will be difficult to scale your earnings as a virtual assistant. There's a ceiling to how much clients you can take. However, it can be scalable if you have your own business wherein several virtual assistants work under you. You can scale the business by hiring more virtual assistants.

   5/10

D. **Competitiveness:**
   The industry where virtual assistants operate is very competitive. There are literally millions of virtual assistants out there, most of whom are from third-world countries in Asia like the Philippines, India, and Pakistan.

   2/10

Tips on How to Be Successful as a Virtual Assistant

- Assess your skills to make sure that you have what it takes to perform your tasks. Basically, if you have experience working as a secretary or assistant in an office setting, then that's a good starting point.

- You must be savvy in using the internet and all the communication tools you need to work for a remote client. You have to be adept in using email, video conferencing sites, chat rooms, Skype, etc.

- You must have the necessary and appropriate equipment. First of all, you must have a fast and reliable internet connection. Other hardware you should have includes a printer, a scanner, a camera, or any other device that your boss requires from you.

- Develop a specialty. It's very difficult to find a job as a virtual assistant if you promote yourself as a jack of all trades. You have to offer a special kind of skill to get the attention of potential employers. For example, you can focus on being a social media specialist, an SEO expert, a travel organizer, etc.

- Don't promise what you can't deliver. In their desperation to get a gig, some virtual assistants exaggerate their capabilities. This is a huge mistake that can return and ruin your reputation for good.

- Do a lot of networking. Many companies and professionals hire virtual assistants using a referral system. This means they hire a person if he or she has been referred or recommended by someone they trust. Needless to say, if you have a lot of connections in the industry, you have a better chance of finding jobs.

- Attend trainings. There are a lot of virtual assistant trainings that are done online. Many of these are also free which means there's absolutely no reason why you shouldn't join any of them from time to time. There are a lot of lessons that you can learn from these free trainings.

- Always be respectful. Whether you are still applying for a position or you have already taken it, always be respectful to your boss. Online jobs are mostly unregulated so there's not much that you can do if an employee suddenly decides to terminate your position.

- Create a schedule. This is very important if you are working for more than one employer. You have to make sure that your schedules don't overlap. Time management is a very important skill that every virtual assistant must have.

- Keep in touch with former employers. They might hire you again or they might refer you to others looking for someone like you. Again, networking is necessary in the industry. The more connections you have, the better it will be for you as a virtual assistant.

Frequently Asked Questions and Answers

- What kind of tasks do virtual assistants perform?
  - It depends on who he/she works for. Sample tasks include handling email, answering remote phone calls, making appointments, doing paperwork, researching information, planning meetings and events, making travel arrangements, handling reservations, writing articles, proofreading content, etc.

- How much can I charge clients for my assistance work?
  - It depends on the pay structure of the deal you entered into. You can be paid by the hour, per task, or per month. Typically, you can charge between $10 to $20 per hour. However, you can charge a lot more if your skills are highly specialized and there aren't many virtual assistants with those skillsets in the market. This is another reason you might consider specializing instead of being a jack of all trade.

- Where can I find virtual assistance jobs?
  - Start your search in job sites like Freelancer, Codeable, Upwork, Guru, and even Craigslist.

- What are the minimum qualities that a virtual assistant must have?
  - Since most of your potential clients will be dealing with you in English, it's important that you have good verbal English skills, written English skills, and organization skills. And of course, you should be familiar with online communication tools like email, Skype etc.

- What tools can I use to make my work as a virtual assistant easier?
  - You must be equipped with tools Skype, Dropbox, Acrobat Connect, Facebook Messenger, Google Apps, LogMeIn, Team Viewer, and other necessary tools and apps.

- How do I get paid as a virtual assistant?
  - There are a variety of ways on how you can get paid. So far, the most popular method is through an online payment provider like Skrill, PayPal and Payoneer. However, you can also be paid through bank transfer and cheques.

- Is it possible to work as a virtual assistant full-time?
  - Yes, of course. There are businesses and entrepreneurs out there who are looking for full-time virtual assistants.

- How do I get started as a virtual assistant?
  - The first step is to create your resume. Don't forget to highlight the information that makes you a good candidate for a virtual assistant position. You then sign up with job sites and look for VA listings. Apply and if they ask for your resume, send it to them.

- How many clients can I have as a virtual assistant?
  - Most virtual assistants maintain more than one clients. This is why it is very important that you learn how to organize your tasks and manage your time. You have to master the art of scheduling your job responsibilities. Having more than one client will also help you diversify your income stream instead of relying solely on one.

- How do I protect myself from clients who turn out to be scammers?
  - Scams are quite common in the industry. The best way to protect yourself is to do your research and ensure that the person or company hiring you is legit. Another strategy is to ask for a retainer fee. That is you get paid a portion of your salary in advance. Sites like upwork.com also have a review system whereby the both the client and the virtual assistants review each other after a project is completed. Clients that are legitimate tend to have good ratings and a long profile history.

Myth Busters About Working as a Virtual Assistant

- That you only need a computer and an internet connection to become a virtual assistant. There's so much more to it than that.

- Working as a virtual assistant is just for work-at-home moms. Not true. The responsibilities of a virtual assistant can be performed by anyone.

- Virtual assistants are employees. This is a misnomer because virtual assistants are independent contractors and self-employed individuals. They work "with" their bosses, not "for" their bosses.

- It's easy money. Nothing can be further from the truth. The tasks of a virtual assistant can be difficult and time-consuming.

- Virtual assistants do not need training. False again. To be an effective virtual assistant, you need to be aware of the ins and outs of the business.

- That the market is too crowded because there are millions of virtual assistants out there. There's no truth to the claim that the market is too crowded. In fact, a lot of companies sometimes find it hard to find an available virtual assistant.

- Virtual assistants all come from India and Pakistan. This is nothing but a stereotype. There are thousands of virtual assistants working from western countries like the United States, Canada, and the United Kingdom.

- That virtual assistants can steal business ideas and data. Yes, there's a possibility but it's rare. Besides, you should never let a virtual assistant have access to your most important and most sensitive data. When outsourcing tasks, only consider those that do not expose sensitive information e.g. bank details etc.

- That virtual assistants only work part-time. Although most virtual assistants work part-time, there's a lot of them who work at it full-time.

- That virtual assistants need some sort of certification. Not true at all. In fact, 90% or more of virtual assistants out there don't have any certification for the simple reason that it's not required by most clients.

Inspiration #7

"All progress takes place outside the comfort zone."

Michael John Bobak

Business #7

Affiliate Marketing

Affiliate marketing follows a really simple business model. You sign up with an affiliate company then promote their products or services. Every time you make a successful sale, you earn a commission. Commissions can range from a few cents to several thousand dollars depending on the commission percentage and selling price of the product. For example, let's say you promoted and sold a product worth $500 with a commission rate of 10%. With that commission percentage, your take from the sale would be a good $50. As you can see, affiliate marketing can be a very lucrative source of passive income if you are very smart about it (i.e. promoting high ticket items or items with backend commissions). Another good thing about affiliate marketing is that there's absolutely no limit to the number of affiliate products you can choose to promote and sell.

The first step in starting an affiliate marketing business is choosing the right platform. The good news is that there are dozens of companies you can choose from. The biggest and most influential of these affiliate marketing companies are Amazon, Clickbank, Rakuten, eBay, and Commission Junction. If you are new in the industry, it's highly recommended that you start with these companies because they already have the reputation and influence. Joining them is much less risky compared to joining new affiliate companies.

Affiliate marketing offers several important benefits to entrepreneurs. One, you don't need to have your own product or service. All you have to do is promote the products of other people and other companies. Two, you don't have to keep inventory or track orders and sales. The product owner or manufacturer handles all these. Again, your sole responsibility is to promote and market the products. Three, there is no cap on the amount of money you can earn. You can earn a few hundred dollars a month or several thousand dollars a day. It's not uncommon for some affiliates to earn as much as six figures in a single month. The point here is that how much you earn depends on how smart and how hard you work on your affiliate marketing business. If you're interested in learning more about this business model, then my book – **Affiliate Marketing: Learn How to Make $10,000+ Month On Autopilot** will interest you. Feel free to listen to a free audio sample here

Ratings Based on Our Criteria

A. **Simplicity:**
   Affiliate marketing requires a good amount of work. You also have to be smart with your product selection, commission/pay structure etc. It may be easy to build a YouTube channel or a website monetized with affiliate products but it takes time to build an audience around it.

   6/10

B. **Passivity:**
   Affiliate marketing remains as one of the best ways on how to generate passive income. If you have a website that's full of valuable evergreen content, it can keep on earning you money even if you don't work on it for weeks or even months.

   8/10

C. **Scalability:**
   It's really easy to scale an affiliate marketing business considering how cheap domain registration and hosting are these days. You can create a dozen affiliate websites that will cost you as low as $100 a month, monetize them with high ticket and relevant affiliate products, drive traffic to them and earn passively. That is truly a bargain. Furthermore, this article gives you some tips you can implement to make sure you're converting as much of that traffic to sales.

   9/10

D. Competitiveness:

This is one of the things you should seriously consider before trying your hands on affiliate marketing. The competition can be very tough especially if you are targeting a very popular niche like personal development or make money online. However, smart niche selection (high demand and low competition e.g. landscaping, gardening etc.) can help you minimize the amount of competition you face. However, if you're very skilled at driving traffic from sources like Facebook ads, YouTube etc. you can do tremendously well regardless of competition.

2/10

Tips on How to Be Successful in Affiliate Marketing

- Focus your attention on products that are relevant to each other. This is very important if you are selling the products through a website or a blog. This strategy is often referred to as niche marketing.

- Promote products that you are knowledgeable about. It's much easier to talk about or write content about products that you know.

- Focus on providing value first, selling the product second. This means writing content that clearly explains to the customer the pros and cons of a product.

- Don't be too aggressive with your sales pitches. Many affiliate marketers fail because their sales tactics are too intrusive.

- Know your audience. This is why research is very important. You have to be fully aware about the needs and wants of your target customers.

- Always be honest and transparent about your affiliate relationships. Don't forget to provide disclosures whenever you are paid directly by a sponsor to write about or recommend a product.

- Try different affiliate programs and see what works well for you. There are dozens of affiliate programs out there. You don't have to use all of them but you should take the time to experiment.

- Write timeless or evergreen content when promoting affiliate products. A piece of content can be considered as timeless and evergreen if it remains relevant and true for years to come.

- Utilize calls to action. Don't be afraid to tell a reader to click here or subscribe there if you are confident about the product you are recommending.

- Always comply with the rules, regulations, and terms of agreement as provided by the program you are using. Weeks or months of hard work can easily go down the drain if the program suddenly terminates your account because you've broken a rule or two.

Frequently Asked Questions and Answers

- How do I make money from affiliate marketing?
  - The affiliate marketing business model is quite simple. You sign up with a company that has an affiliate program like Amazon. You promote their products. If you make a sale, you earn an affiliate commission.

- How do I get started in affiliate marketing?

- The first step is to learn everything you can about affiliate marketing and how it works. My book on Affiliate Marketing will help you with this. However, if you are confident that you have the proper knowledge to get started, you can sign up with a company that offers an affiliate program like Amazon, eBay, and Commission Junction.

- How long until I start making money from affiliate marketing?
  - It depends. It can be a day, it can be weeks, it can be months, and it can even be years. It depends on a lot of factors.

- How do I get paid as an affiliate?
  - It depends on the affiliate marketing company you joined. For example, Amazon pays its affiliates through any of the following options: direct bank deposit, gift certificate (GC), and check. Other affiliate companies pay their marketers via online payment platforms like PayPal, Payoneer, and even crypto-currencies such as Bitcoin.

- What is a niche?
  - The term "niche" is something you will constantly encounter in affiliate marketing. In the simplest of terms, a niche is a specific topic or theme which serves as the focus of your marketing efforts. For example, let's say that you have an affiliate marketing website that sells soccer memorabilia. In this case, your niche is "soccer memorabilia".

- Do I need a website to make money in affiliate marketing?
  - Not necessarily. There are affiliate marketers who are still able to generate a decent amount of affiliate income although they don't have a website or a blog (i.e. they could have a YouTube channel with an established audience. They could focus on doing product reviews and posting affiliate links in the video description section). However, getting your own website is very important. With a website, you can double or even triple your chances of making it as an affiliate marketer. It's all about strategically increasing your footprint in the online world i.e. Facebook, YouTube, Instagram, Twitter, Your Website etc.

- Which affiliate marketing company or program should I join?
  - There are literally hundreds of affiliate marketing companies and programs out there. It's advisable that if you are just starting out, you should go with the more established companies. These include Amazon, Terra Leads, Clickbank, Rakuten, Shareasale, eBay Partner Network, Commission Factory, Avangate, and Revenue Wire.

- Do I need to pay taxes?
  - You will have to consult with an accountant because taxation of online earnings differ from one country to another. You need advice on how to declare your online earnings.

- What kind of products can I promote through affiliate marketing?
  - You can promote pretty much anything as long as it's not illegal. You can promote both digital and physical products. There's no shortage of products that you can promote. Amazon alone has millions of products in its marketplace.

- How do I succeed as an affiliate marketer?
  - Succeeding in affiliate marketing is a combination of promoting high-quality products, high-ticket products and strategically driving traffic to your affiliate offers. This free webinar by the legendary online marketer, Kevin David, will show you the power of Facebook Ads for identifying ideal customers for your affiliate products.

Myth Busters About Affiliate Marketing

- That affiliate marketing is a walk in the park. Many people fail in affiliate marketing because they expect it to be a cakewalk. The truth is it requires a lot of work.

- That more traffic equals more affiliate income. Higher traffic definitely helps but it's just one part of the equation. The quality of the traffic is more important than its quantity and the quality is determined by how relevant the offers you promote are to the people you expose the offer to and whether they trust you. After all, people buy from people they know, like and trust.

- That affiliate marketing is more about luck than skill. This is completely false. Affiliate marketing is just like any business. You must have the skills to run it and make it profitable.

- That affiliate marketing is only for professionals with advanced business degrees. You don't need a degree to be successful in affiliate marketing. In fact, most affiliate marketers don't have business degrees.

- That affiliate marketing is all about advertising. Affiliate marketing is more on creating valuable content that convinces people to purchase products.

- That social media popularity can easily translate into affiliate marketing success. That's not always the case.

- That affiliate marketing is a dead end. Affiliate marketing has been around for decades and continues to grow strong. There's absolutely no reason to think that it's a dead end.

- That affiliate marketing is dependent on content posted on a website. Website content is just one aspect of affiliate marketing. You can also leverage YouTube and popular social media platforms like Facebook.

- That it's too late to get engaged in affiliate marketing. It's never too late.

- That you need a lot of money to get started. Nope, you can even start without spending a single penny. However, it'll take longer to gain scale your business.

Inspiration #8

"Don't let the fear of losing be greater than the excitement of winning."
Robert Kiyosaki

Business #8

Dropshipping

The business model for dropshipping is quite simple. You set up a business website where you list down products for sale. However, these products are actually not your products although you make it look like they are yours. You have made a deal with a product manufacturer or supplier that they will ship the products to the customers who buy from your website. That means you are not holding the inventory for the products. You just have them listed on your website. Below is a quick overview of how dropshipping works:

- You find a product manufacturer or supplier and enter into a deal with them. The deal should basically state that you will be dropshipping their products.
- You build a business website and create listings of the products.
- A customer visits your website and decides to purchase a product from you.
- Notified of the purchased item, you then make an order from your manufacturer or supplier.
- The manufacturer or supplier receives the order, processes it, puts it in a package, and ships it to the customer.
- The customer receives the package as if it came from you although it actually came directly from a supplier.

As you can see, there are obvious benefits to this business model. First of all, you don't need to have your own products to create a dropshipping business. You are merely going to promote products by other people and other companies. That means you don't have to go through product development, product testing, and product manufacturing. This also means you don't have to spend huge amounts of cash that are required in making products. In short, there is very little investment on your part. The manufacturer or supplier you entered into a contract with has done the hard work of making the product. You only need to promote it.

You also don't need to keep inventory. Your only worry lies on the orders that are made through your business website. You have to make sure that the orders are immediately forwarded to the supplier so that these can be processed and shipped as soon as possible. So the bottom line here is that your responsibilities as the owner of a dropshipping business are composed of the following simple things:

- List products on your website.
- Process orders then forward these to your supplier.
- Maintain the website.
- That's basically it.

Ratings Based on Our Criteria

A. **Simplicity:**

I would describe dropshipping as very simple because you can pretty much automate the whole thing. As long as your online store is set up, there's not much else that you do. The only challenge here is learning how to effectively drive traffic to your website/online store.

8/10

B. **Passivity:**

Always remember that in dropshipping, you don't own the products and you don't ship them as well. In addition, the money you make is nearly all profits. However, you still have to deal with customer support issues when they arise.

8/10

C. **Scalability:**
Scaling a dropshipping business is a matter of either adding more products to your inventory or creating another online store.

9/10

D. **Competitiveness:**
The dropshipping scene is not as saturated as other online markets only because not many people are aware of the business model. You should expect the industry to become more competitive in the coming years as more people try their luck in building businesses online.

5/10

Tips For Success

- Sell products that you are actually interested in. Why? Because it will be much easier to nurture loyal and repeat customers if you're personally invested in the products you are selling.

- Choose a niche that you are passionate about. It's easier to build a dropshipping business if you enjoy running and managing it. In addition, if you're passionate about your niche then chances are you'll understand your customer avatar better and this will be reflected in the quality of traffic you'll drive to your online store.

- Look for light and durable products to sell. They are easier to sell and there's less risk of breakage etc. when shipping them overseas.

- Don't just build a dropshipping business, build a brand. Make people feel like they are getting something special when they purchase a product from you.

- High quality presentation of your merchandise is very important. Put yourself in the shoes of your potential customers. If you see ugly and unprofessional product photos, would you trust the merchant selling them?

- Establish a good relationship with your supplier and manufacturer. This ensures that you'll more or less get the products whenever you need them. Burning bridges in the dropshipping industry can easily wipe out your operations.

- See to it that your pricing policy is reasonable. The general rule is that you should not underprice nor overprice your products. Underpricing creates the impression that your product are low quality. Overpricing, on the other hand, can turn off customers.

- Ensure availability for all of your products. Nothing disappoints a customer more than learning that the product he badly wants is out of stock.

- Automate certain aspects of your business. There are so many apps that you can use to make it easier to run your dropshipping business. You should take advantage of these tools.

- Offer exceptional customer service. A lot of things can go wrong in a dropshipping business. A supplier may not keep his end of the bargain. The package arrives late. There are bugs in the ordering and payment system. These are just a few of the common problems associated with dropshipping. Make sure that you deal with them as soon as possible to keep your customers happy.

Frequently Asked Questions and Answers

- What kind of profit margin can I expect from dropshipping?
  - Your profit margin will depend greatly on the products that you are selling and the suppliers you are getting them from. Average profit margins are in the 5% to 10% range. However, for some low-priced items such as accessories, profit margins can go as high as 90%.

- Do I need to buy the products before I sell them?
  - No, that's absolutely not necessary. That is the beauty of dropshipping. You only purchase the products from your supplier or manufacturer when a customer orders them. This means you can sell hundreds of products while your supplier scrambles to ship them to your customers.

- Do I need a website to be successful in dropshipping?
  - Yes, you need to set up a website in the form of an online store. There should be a place where customers can browse through your products and purchase them if they want them. If you are not a web developer, there are online tools and apps that you can use to get an online store. For example, you can sign up with Shopify, an online service that allows you to create a complete dropshipping website in minutes.

- Do I need a supplier?
  - Yes. You are in the dropshipping business which means you don't make the products yourself. This also means that you need a supplier or a manufacturer to provide you with the products you are going to sell.

- How do I find a supplier?
  - Google is your best friend here. There are dozens of marketplaces online where you can find suppliers for any product you fancy. Such marketplaces include SaleHoo, Dropship Direct, Whosesale Central, Inventory Source, Alibaba, AliExpress, Doba, Worldwide Brands, and Megagoods.

- What kind of fees do dropshipping companies charge?
  - Aside from the cost of the products you are dropshipping, companies may also charge you pre-order fees and monthly fees. It's quite common for companies to charge pre-order fees to cover the costs involved in packaging and shipping an individual product. Companies may also charge you a monthly fee for the privilege of doing business with them.

- What are the requirements in starting a dropshipping business?
  - The requirements differ based on the country where you are headquartered. In the United States, you need to incorporate your business with your state. You need to request for an EIN number from the IRS. You need to request for a sales and tax ID from your state.

- Who takes care of customer service in a business that follows the dropshipping model?
  - The responsibility is on you as the retailer. You have to handle support issues, solve problems, and deal with any other issue that arises form customer complaints. Your supplier simply ships the products to your customers. That's their only responsibility.

- How much money do I need to get started?
  - It depends on several factors. Some dropshipping businesses can be started with just $100 while some require more than $1000. It depends on the products you are selling, the costs of shipping your products, the tools you are using, etc.

- How do I attract customers to my dropshipping store?

- There are a lot of ways. You can do social media marketing, direct advertising, blogging, and search engine optimization among others.

Myth Busters About Dropshipping

- That dropshipping only works for low-priced general products. It's not true. Dropshipping works for all kinds of products and price bands.

- That you need to be tech-savvy and a coding expert to be engaged in dropshipping. This is not a requirement. You can easily outsource the design of your website to freelance web developers on upwork or fiverr who will handle that for you.

- That you can make money overnight. Dispel this notion from your mind. Like any worthwhile business, it takes time to achieve notable success. This is not a get rich quick scheme.

- That dropshipping only involves listing products in a website. That's not true. You still have to process and forward orders to your suppliers and handle customer service when necessary e.g. a customer returning a faulty product etc.

- That dropshipping is very expensive and only a few people can afford it. This is not entirely true. Some dropshipping businesses can be started with just $100 while some require more than $1000. It depends on the products you are selling, the costs of shipping your products, the tools you are using, etc.

- That dropshipping is a saturated niche and that it's too late to get into the industry. It's never too late. The demand for consumer products continue to grow and with the right product selection, you can carve out a profitable niche for yourself.

- That dropshipping is a scam. If you don't do your due diligence i.e. research the suppliers you work with, their reputation, trade history etc. then you may be scammed.

- That dropshipping is only about exporting low-quality products from China. This is entirely false as you can dropship quality products manufactured in Europe or USA for that matter.

- That dropshipping is too confusing for ordinary entrepreneurs. It depends on the person. Yes, there's always a learning curve. However, there are ebooks, courses online and mentors you can work with to provide guidance when required.

- That if your supplier runs out of stock, you are toast. This is not true. You can minimize the risk of this occurring by diversifying i.e. partnering with multiple suppliers

Inspiration #9

"If you really look closely, most overnight successes took a long time."

Steve Jobs

Business #9

Create Online Courses

There is an immense market for all sorts of online courses. It doesn't matter what kind of course it is, there's always a group of people out there who will find the course helpful and valuable. How to plant and raise roses. How to paint using ground coffee beans. How to create a mobile application. How to make money from your YouTube videos. How to write and independently publish a novel. How to draw anime. How to create your own wedding dress.

These are just a few examples of simple but valuable ideas for courses that can find a profitable audience online. If you are good at something, there's a good chance that you can earn passive income from it by creating an online course around it.

If you are knowledgeable or skilled about a certain topic, creating a course about it should be a breeze. Even better is the fact that there are online platforms which allow you to make these online courses with ease. Udemy comes to mind. This is basically a company whose core service is to help people make courses and connect them with their target audiences. Udemy is just one of several companies that offer this type of service. With that said, you should take the time to explore other platforms to find the ones that are most appropriate to your brand of courses. But if you are just staring out in the business of making and selling online courses, Udemy would be a good place to start. They offer you a variety of tools and resources that will make your life a lot easier.

If you don't want to make use of third-party service providers like Udemy, you can always sell your courses directly to your target customers. The best way to do this is to make your course downloadable so that a paying customer can access them within a few minutes. It will be more difficult to find customers this way because you have to be aggressive in your marketing efforts. But if you are confident in your marketing skills, then go for it. It's important that you create a website or a blog which will serve as your main marketing machine. It's where you direct people who might be interested in your course.

To promote your courses, you should combine a lot of online marketing strategies like search engine optimization, video marketing, content marketing, direct advertising, and social media marketing. The last one (social media marketing) can be very effective if you learn how to leverage advertising programs by social networking sites. For example, Facebook has its own advertising program. What's great about Facebook's advertising program is that you can customize your campaign so that your ad will only reach the types of people you want to reach. You can customize your target audience by geographical location, by gender, by age, and by their hobbies and interests. It's a very efficient way to find people who are genuinely interested in your online courses.

Ratings Based on Our Criteria

A. **Simplicity:**
   I wouldn't call the business model simple given the fact that building an online course from scratch can be quite complicated. It requires a lot of research and writing. However, sites like Udemy, Thinkific and Teachable have done a lot to simplify the process.

   6/10

B. **Passivity:**
   Once the hard work of creating the course is over, there's not much work left aside from promoting the course. Most of the profits from this point on are mostly passive in nature.

   8/10

C. **Scalability:**

To scale, you just have to increase your marketing budget to reach more people. This free webinar by the legendary online marketer, Kevin David, will show you the power of Facebook Ads for identifying ideal customers for your online course. You can also create another online course. It's like writing a book on top of another. The more courses you have circulating, the more passive income you make.

9/10

D. **Competitiveness:**

Competition depends on your niche. If you are offering a course in a very popular niche, then the competition can be very tough. This is why before you start creating a course, make sure that the market is not already saturated with courses similar to what you have in mind. However, if you're very good with Facebook advertising, YouTube advertising or marketing in general, then you have a considerable edge over your competitors.

4/10

Tips For Success

- Choose the perfect course topic. This means that the topic should be something that you love and something that you are actually knowledgeable in. It's much easier to build a course if you know what you are talking about.

- Perform some research to ensure that your course idea has high market demand. No matter how good your course is if nobody out there wants it, you're not going to make any money from it.

- Create a compelling presentation of the learning outcomes or the kind of transformation people can expect after going through your course. What are they going to get from it? Where can they apply the things they learn from your courses?

- Structure your course modules. The general rule in structuring a course is to start with the simplest lessons then slowly graduate to the more advanced lessons. The goal in every module is to prepare the learner for the next module.

- Gather content for your course from reputable sources. If you are going to cite someone in your course, make sure that he's someone who is considered as an expert in the field.

- Make it as easy as possible for the learner to access your course. It should be as easy as downloading a file or logging into a website.

- Make your course as engaging as possible by combining all types of media (text, video, audio, infographics, etc.)

- Promote your course in every platform possible. Promote it in your social media networks. Promote it through email marketing. Promote it in your blog. Promote it in your podcast. Just get your name out there.

- Create a whole series of courses. This is a great way to nurture your customers and build a following. This business model is similar to writing a book series. You keep giving your customers something to look forward to.

- Collaborate with other online course creators. You get to use each other as leverage to increase your customer base.

Frequently Asked Questions and Answers

- What is an online course?
  - It's a course which is delivered to learners online. It can be in the form of a series of articles, video tutorials, presentations, or even live lessons.

- Where can I sell an online course I created?
  - You can market the course directly to your target audience. You can use platforms like Udemy, Teachable, Thinkific, Skillshare, LearnWorlds, CourseCraft, etc.

- What is Udemy?
  - This is just one of several online platforms where you can create and sell your online courses.

- What kind of online course can I make?
  - You can make any course you want as long as you're knowledgeable about the topic being discussed and there's a market for it.

- How do I promote my online courses?
  - Use a variety of proven online marketing techniques likes search engine optimization, social media marketing, email marketing and advertising.

- What's the cost of creating a course?
  - It depends on several factors. These factors include the platform that you are using, the tools you are using to create the course, and if you are hiring other people to help you in making the course. That being said, you can create a course on Thinkific for free (as of July 2018).

- How much money can I earn from my courses?
  - Again, it depends on a lot of factors. But for inspiration, you should know that there are some course creators who earn up to six figures a month.

- Do I have to be a coder to create a course?
  - Not necessarily. There are some courses that you can create without any coding skills. You can also hire someone to handle the technical aspects of creating the course. Online course platforms like Teachable and Thinkific have so simplified the process that anyone can create a course.

- What tools do I need to create an online course?
  - It depends on the kind of course you are making. Is it a video course? Then you need video-editing tools and software like Screenflow, Camtasia etc.

- How do I deliver my online courses to clients?
  - The best way is to provide them with a downlink link.

Myth Busters About Creating Online Courses

- That you have to be an expert in something before you can make a course about it. You don't need to be an expert to create an online course. As long as you are know enough to teach other people who may be slightly below you in the learning curve you're within your rights to create a course. If anything, your audience will relate more to you and your course because you understand their pain points better having been there yourself not too long ago. Its one thing knowing something and another thing being able to teach it in a way people can understand.

- That you have to choose a course that is currently trending. This is false. Trending or not, all you simply have to do is choose a topic that has proven demand and you have some experience with it.

- That you shouldn't create a course around a topic if there are already existing courses about it. Again, this is not true. The fact other courses exist doesn't mean they do a good job addressing the issue. If you believe you have something to offer you should give it a go.

- That the tech stuff is so difficult that only develops are able to perform them. Platforms like Udemy, Teachable and Thinkific have made the course creation process so easy anybody with enough motivation can do it.

- That creating a course is very expensive. Once again, this is far from the truth given that you can create an online course with platforms like Thinkific for free.

- That you are required to be in front of the camera and talk to people. Being in front of a camera is not strictly required. You can tailor the course to suit your teaching style – talking over a presentation slide, showing a video of yourself delivering the course etc.

- That no one will buy your course because people can just Google it. This is not true as people purchase courses to achieve a given aim or transformation in as short a time as possible. Not everyone has the time to sieve through all the information on the internet to find the ones that are specifically tailored to them – that's the purpose of a course.

- That you need thousands of people in your email list before you can launch a course. This is not entirely true. It's more about the quality of the email list rather then the quantity. If you have a good relationship with the people on your email list and they know you, like you and trust you then you're golden. You build relationship by giving value first then selling later.

- That no one will purchase your course if you increase the price due to upgrades. There'll always be a small section of your customers who will be interested in purchasing your premium products as long as they offer something of equal value. It's advisable to have different price tiers/packages to cater to as many of your customers as possible.

- That you need to create lots and lots of courses to be able to earn real income from teaching courses. This is not necessarily true. Yes, you may need a lot of courses to scale but earning a real income comes from creating valuable content and marketing them well. This will allow you to charge a premium price, which means you don't need to sell a lot to make a significant income.

Inspiration #10

"The way to get started is to quit talking and begin doing."

Walt Disney

Business #10

Build an Application

It's not uncommon to hear about apps that earn their creators thousands of dollars every month. Hell, there are even app creators who became millionaires through simple but helpful applications. If you have good coding and programming skills that can be translated to app development, or you know how to hire good freelance programmers that'll develop apps for you then this is an industry you should explore. The market for apps, especially mobile apps, is at an all-time high. With more and more people getting connected to the internet through their smartphones, the market for apps will only grow bigger and even more lucrative. For sure, the app development sector is unbelievably competitive but there are new opportunities that are always emerging.

You can build an app from scratch or you can build one using an open-source software. Each strategy has its own pros and cons so it's up to you to choose the method that will work best for you. Take advantage of the tools and resources that are available online to build and polish your app. And before you launch and offer your app for download, make sure that you have tested it several times. A single bug (i.e. malfunction) in the app can easily destroy all your hard work. It's difficult to get a second chance in the app development field. So make sure that you get it right the first time.

After creating and extensively testing your app, the next step is to market it to the world. Your first move should be to have your app listed in popular app stores. This will expose your app to thousands of potential customers. If your app is good enough, people will start talking about it and that's where word-of-mouth starts. If your app offers something of value, it should be able to market itself. However, this doesn't mean that you just sit back and let your app do all the self-promotion stuff. You are setting yourself up for failure if this is your attitude.

No matter how good you think your app is, you still have to spend tons of your time and resources in promoting and marketing it. Create a page for it on Facebook. Endlessly talk about it on Twitter or Instagram. Purchase ads for it in technology websites and blogs. Do some email marketing. The point here is that you should put yourself out there and do everything that you can to let people know about your new app.

Ratings Based on Our Criteria

A. **Simplicity:**
   Hey, building an application is not easy. You must have the educational background as well as the technical experience to create one from scratch or, at the very least, know how to hire people with the necessary expertise to build one for you (which will probably cost you).

   5/10

B. **Passivity:**
   Once the app is up for grabs, pretty much most of the income you generate are passive in nature.

   8/10

C. **Scalability:**
   It can be hard to scale an app business if you are operating solo. But if you are working within a team wherein you have the capability to develop several apps at the same time, then scalability can easily be achieved.

   7/10

D. **Competitiveness:**

The app business is very hot right now so the competition can be fierce. You are competing not just against individual developers but against app-building companies that are backed by millions of dollars in funding.

1/10

Tips For Success

- Outline your app's purpose before you even get started with the coding process. This will save you a lot of time and money down the road. What is your app for? What kind of value will people get from it? When you have a clear answer to these questions, then that's the time you get started.

- Clearly identify the potential market for your app. If there's no market then there's no money to be made. Try asking your friends and family if your idea of an app is something they might be interested in.

- Keep it simple. Don't you notice that majority of the most successful apps out there are often the most simple ones? It's because people need simplicity not complexity.

- Make your app compatible with as many operating systems as possible. If your app is only available in one operating system, then you are limiting your app's potential.

- Test your app several times before you launch. A launch that's riddled with errors and bugs can quickly ruin all your hard work. So test your app over and over again until you are completely sure that it's working properly and smoothly.

- Less is more. Many developers often make the mistake of assuming that an app becomes better as you add more features to it. Just identify the problem you are trying to solve and make it the focus of your app.

- Make your app free. Obviously, this strategy is not for everyone but it's a strategy you should consider. Making your app free can double and even triple the attention that your app gets. You make money by offering in-app purchases, selling advertising space or offering a paid version of your app that has no ads. Be creative

- Marketing is everything. You should come up with a plan on how you are going to promote your app.

- Think like a user. During the entirety of the development process, always look at your app with the perspective of your potential user. If you don't like what you are creating, then your user will probably think the same.

- Seek feedback from other experienced app developers. Ask them what they think of your app. Take their comments and use these to build an even better app.

Frequently Asked Questions and Answers

- How much does it cost to build a mobile application?
    - It depends on the size and nature of the app. Some apps can cost $5000 and some can cost six figures.

- How long does it take to develop a mobile app?
    - Again, it depends on the size and nature of the app. Some apps can be built in a few days and some can take months or even years.

- How do I validate my app idea?
  - You have to perform extensive research to determine if there's going to be a market for your app. Do similar apps exist and are people paying for them or at the very least downloading them?

- What is the best way to monetize an app?
  - Aside from selling the app on a per download basis, you can also offer in-app purchases. This is a great strategy especially for gaming apps.

- Should I develop apps using Android or iOS?
  - If you are skilled in both, you should use both to widen your potential market.

- How do I get more app downloads?
  - You have to promote and market it like crazy. Use every imaginable marketing platform like social media sits, forums, and app stores.

- How do I market my app?
  - Sign up with as many app stores as you can and have your app listed in them. You should also promote your app in social media, blogs, YouTube and on your own website.

- How many times do I have to test my app before launching it?
  - Keep testing it until you don't see any bugs or flaws in it.

- Can I still have an app created even if I'm not a developer?
  - Yes, of course. This is where freelance app developers enter the picture. You come up with the app idea and the developer will execute it for you. You can hire freelancers from Upwork, Fiverr etc.

- Is it a good idea to offer my app for free?
  - Yes, if it's a marketing strategy. You can offer free download and usage for a certain period of time. Or you can simply give away the app but monetize it through in-app purchases.

Myth Busters About Building and Making Money from Apps

- That mobile apps are cheap. We have already established that it'll depends on the nature of the app you want to build.

- That mobile apps are for smartphones only. This is not true. Normal phones still have mobile apps like Gmail, Google map etc.

- That you can be an instant millionaire after developing an app. While this is possible, it's highly unlikely. Nothing worthwhile happens instantly, there's always a learning process.

- That app development is a one-time thing. This is not true, as you need still need to listen to customer feedback, provide updates/upgrades to keep your customers happy and the app competitive.

- That you need to be a developer to have a functioning app created. This is far from the truth. If you have no technical skills, you can hire freelancers to develop apps for you.

- That developing native apps for each platform is impractical. It's practical if the have the necessary resources and technical know-how

- That the release of an app ends its development. Not true. You still have to look at customer feedback/review and work on releasing updates/upgrades to keep your app competitive.

- That mobile app development is just coding and nothing else. This is not true. A lot of marketing is required after the app is launched

- That you can build a perfect app for all platforms in a single attempt. While this is possible, it's highly unlikely.

- That your app can get thousands of users without any marketing. I think we both know by now this is not true. Regardless of how good the app is, you'll need to market it, get the word out and raise awareness. If your app happens to be very valuable, word of mouth marketing may eventually kick in which will save you a lot of marketing spend.

Inspiration #11
"The successful warrior is the average man, with laser-like focus."
Bruce Lee

Series #	Book Title
1	Affiliate Marketing
2	Passive Income Ideas
3	Affiliate Marketing + Passive Income Ideas (2-in-1 Bundle)
4	Facebook Advertising
5	Dropshipping
6	Dropshipping + Facebook Advertising (2-in-1 Bundle)
7	Real Estate Investing For Beginners
8	Credit Cards and Credit Repair Secrets
9	Real Estate Investing And Credit Repair Strategies (2-in-1 Bundle)
10	Passive Income Ideas With Affiliate Marketing (2nd Edition)
11	Passive Income With Dividend Investing
12	Stock Market Investing For Beginners
13	The Simple Stock Market Investing Blueprint (2-in-1 Bundle)
14	Real Estate And Stock Market Investing Mastery (3-in-1 Bundle)

15	Amazon FBA Mastery

Business #11

Online Consultancy

Are you an expert in something? Maybe you are a pro in Adobe Photoshop. Maybe you are skilled in creating Facebook pages that pop. Maybe you have years of experience in social media marketing. Maybe you are adept in business law and taxation. If you are skilled in something, you should consider offering your knowledge as an online consultant. What's great about this business model is that anyone from anywhere in the world can become your client. Maybe there's a business student in London who needs your business law expertise. Maybe there's a company CEO in Japan who wants you to teach him how to optimize his company's Facebook page. The point here is that if you're good at something, you can create an income source from it by simply offering advice to people.

Online consultancy is a very competitive niche so you should be smart which fields or industries you enter. Getting clients for your consultancy business is all about proving to your potential customers that you are who they're looking for. You have to show them that you got the goods. Aside from providing samples or testaments to your previous work, you also have to constantly work on your personal branding. You have to get your name out there. The best way to do that is to keep on providing exceptional services to your clients.

To get the word out about your services, you must have a website, a blog, and a social media presence. These are the platforms that you are going to use to promote yourself to your target audience. The more you use them, the more people will know about you and your consulting business.

Ratings Based on Our Criteria

A. **Simplicity:**
   Online consultancy can be an easy and simple job if you are genuinely passionate about it. If you like helping people out, the job can be fun and enjoyable.

   8/10

B. **Passivity:**
   As an online consultant, you are usually paid by the hour or with a fixed monthly pay. This is not exactly the definition of passive income. However, you can make it passive by structuring the deal with your clients so that you can get a certain portion of their profits, company i.e. stock option or royalties in exchange for helping them improve their bottom line. Dan Kennedy is one person I know who has successfully implemented such a strategy.

   5/10

C. **Scalability:**
   It's hard to scale a gig like online consultancy for the simple reason that you have limited time and resources as a singular person. Of course, you can scale the business by starting a firm where you hire other consultants to work under you and charge a premium for clients to work directly with you.

   In addition, you can use the Facebook ad platform to identify the ideal clients for your business and put your offer directly in front of them. This free webinar by the legendary online marketer, Kevin David, shows you how this can be achieved.

   6/10

D. **Competitiveness:**
   The online consultancy arena is full of competitors especially if you operate within a saturated niche. For example, if you plan on becoming a social media consultant, be prepared because you will be competing with thousands of other social media consultants out there.

3/10

Tips For Success

- Offer free consultations. This is a very powerful strategy if you are just starting out. Getting your first clients is one of the hardest parts of online consulting. Offering free consultations is a good way to get the ball rolling.

- Leverage your existing network. Again, this is a powerful strategy if you are just starting out. Reach out to your friends and colleagues if they know of someone who might be in need of your consulting services.

- Learn how to approach potential clients. Yes, this sounds rather intrusive but it works. If you are confident with what you are offering, then there's no reason why you should be afraid to directly approach potential clients.

- Connect with influencers in your niche. The relationships you build with well-known names in your niche have a huge impact on your reputation and brand.

- Leverage social networks that are tailored to professionals and business-minded people. The biggest of these networks is LinkedIn so make sure that you have an account there.

- Try offering free webinars. A webinar is a seminar that's done online. It's basically a videoconference where you get to speak to dozens or even hundreds of people. This is another great way to get your name out there.

- Focus on building relationships, not revenues. The thinking behind this is that if you build relationships first and sell later, the revenue will follow. To be successful in consulting, you must have an army of loyal and repeat clients.

- Familiarize yourself with the competition. Are they offering something that you don't? Are they getting more clients than you? What are they doing to be so successful? Learn from them and implement what you learn in your own consultancy services.

- Be active on social media platforms. Be on Facebook. Be on Twitter. Be on Instagram. Hundreds of your potential clients are active users of these sites.

- Regularly get in touch with your clients. Call them if you have to. Ask them for updates about the projects that you helped them with. A quick call or a simple email message can do wonders in rekindling the business relationship you have with former clients.

Frequently Asked Questions and Answers

- What do online consultants do?
  - They have similar responsibilities as offline consultants. It's just that everything is done remotely on the internet.

- How do I become an online consultant?
  - Do you have a skill or expertise that you think people will pay you for? If your answer is yes, then you can become an online consultant.

- Do I have to sign up with a consultancy agency?
  - It depends on your preferences. You can sign up with an agency or you can offer your services directly to clients.

- How much can I earn as an online consultant?
  - It depends in your niche and the amount of time you spend on the job. You can earn a full-time income from online consultancy if you work hard for it. If you become exceptionally good at it and build a strong reputation, you can charge pretty much what you want. Think of people like Dan Kennedy!

- Where do I find clients?
  - Browse job sites and classified ads sites. Take note of individual entrepreneurs or businesses looking for consultants.

- How do I get paid?
  - Most online consultants are paid through an online payment service like PayPal and Payoneer.

- Do I have to pay taxes?
  - It depends on the country you are located. If you are based in the United States, yes you definitely need to disclose your earnings and pay the corresponding taxes.

- Is it necessary to create my own website?
  - It's not a requirement per se but it can help you a lot if you have your own website.

- How do I charge my clients?
  - You decide how you want to get paid. You can charge per hour or per project.

- How do I promote my online consulting services?
  - Same as what you would do when marketing anything online. Blogging, social media marketing, SEO, advertising, etc.

Myth Busters About Online Consultancy

- That you can earn a lot of money doing very little work. You can ONLY when you have established yourself, clients know your reputation for delivering results and you have a notable brand.

- That you should have a business degree before you can do online consulting. This is not a requirement. As long as you have experience with something and you can leverage that experience to help others you can be a consultant.

- That online consulting is only for experts in their fields. It depends on your definition of on expert. As long as you have a personal experience and knowledge about something, you can be a consultant. You don't need a fancy degree or certificate to qualify. If you can get results for your clients you're golden.

- That it's very easy to find jobs as an online consultant. It's not (at least at the very beginning when you're still trying to establish yourself). You have to put yourself out there. Get on social media platforms, business sites like LinkedIn etc. Market yourself.

- That you don't have to pay taxes because most of your responsibilities are performed online. This is not true. Depending on the country where you operate, you may have to declare your earnings. We advise speaking to your accountant to better understand what your options are.

- That online consulting is full of scammers. Every business opportunity has its fair share of scammers. You have to do your due diligence to ensure people you hire to help you are actually capable of doing what they say they're going to do. Look to reviews, personal reference, free consultation to gauge their skill level/knowledge etc.

- That online consulting is a saturated field and that it's too late to join the industry. The online consulting industry continues to grow strongly and there's plenty of opportunity for success as long as you market yourself correctly.

- That online consulting is only for work-at-home moms. This is not true. Anybody who has experience with something and can help others with that knowledge can become a consultant

- That you can't make a full-time income from online consulting alone. That's not true at all. On the contrary, you can make a full time living as a consultant. If there's a demand for what you offer and you market yourself well, you can thrive in this industry. Look to people like Dan Kennedy for inspiration!

- That entrepreneurs and businesses aren't in need of consultants because they can just Google solutions for their problems. That's far from the truth. Serious business people value their time. They most likely won't waste it searching the web for answers. Besides, with a consultant, they get answers that are specifically tailored to their situation and, in some cases, ongoing support from someone who understands their business.

Inspiration #12

"There are no secrets to success. It is the result of preparation, hard work, and learning from failure."
Colin Powell

Business #12

Online Surveys

I'm going to be brutally honest with you here and tell you right now that you can earn good money from online surveys but don't expect such amounts to be consistent. You should only treat online surveys as a complimentary source of income. There are days wherein there's a good amount of surveys. But there are also days wherein there are zero surveys to accomplish. Of course, this depends on the survey company but this is always the trend within the online surveys niche.

How you make money from online surveys is pretty simple. You sign up with a survey company, log into their surveys dashboard to see if there are any surveys available, accomplish them, and get paid for your efforts. Some surveys can be worth a few cents. Some can be worth three figures. These surveys are usually questionnaires about products, services, and trends. A lot of these are done by companies for market research purposes.

There are dozens of survey companies out there that you can join. These include Swagbucks, Toluna, MySurvey, YouGov, Panel Opinion, Survey Bods, Hiving, Prolific Academic, Global test Market, PanelBase, Pinecone ResearchOpinion Outpost, and so much more. How you get paid depends on the survey company. Some pay in cash via PayPal, some pay through bank transfer, and some pay through rewards in the form of coupons, gift cards, and discounts on certain products and services.

To earn a nice amount of money from online surveys, you need to constantly check your dashboards to see if there are surveys available. You should also be constantly checking your email because many survey companies inform their members of new surveys through email.

Ratings Based on Our Criteria

A. **Simplicity:**
   Making money from online surveys is very simple. Most of the questions are answerable by a yes or a no. Furthermore, majority of the surveys are in multiple choice formats.

   8/10

B. **Passivity:**
   Technically speaking, money you earn from online surveys are far away from being passive. If you complete a survey, you get paid for it. And it stops there. You don't earn additional income from surveys that you've already completed. Unless you have bots or virtual assistants hired to answer surveys on your behalf there's little you can do to make this passive. That being said, you can focus some of your time in referring friends. Many survey companies have their own referral programs. This means you get a cut from the earnings of those people you referred to the website. All in all, this is more a make money online option rather than a passive income opportunity.

   2/10

C. **Scalability:**
   The number of surveys you are given are controlled by the survey companies. Even if you want to scale your earnings, there's very little thing that you can do. You just complete what's given to you. That being said, you can scale to a certain extent by working with more survey companies to ensure there's always a steady stream of surveys to complete.

   5/10

D. **Competitiveness:**

To be honest, the online survey industry has already reached a saturation point. There are too many people willing to complete surveys but there's not enough surveys to go round.

1/10

Tips For Success

- Sign up with as many paid survey sites as possible. As I've mentioned above, survey companies don't always have surveys available. So if the available survey in one company runs out, you can always log into the other companies if there are surveys available.

- Make sure that the survey company is legit before you sign up. There are a lot of fake websites out there that present themselves as survey sites but they're actually not survey sites.

- Fill out your profile completely. You see, a lot of the surveys that will be available to you are dependent on the information that you have entered into your profile.

- Be smart and honest when answering screening questions. Sometimes, before you gain access to a survey, you are required to answer screening questions. You should answer the questions as truthfully as possible.

- Don't rush through the surveys. Keep in mind that some surveys won't pay you if your answers are riddled with inconsistencies.

- Regularly check your email inbox for updates on the latest surveys. If you are using Gmail, you should create a folder where all your survey emails will be redirected to.

- Take the survey as soon as you are notified of it. Once you receive a survey, complete it immediately before someone else does.

- Focus some of your time in referring friends. Many survey companies have their own referral programs. This means you get a cut from the earnings of those people you referred to the website.

- Get a PayPal account. This is very important because most survey sites pay their members through PayPal. Getting an account is super easy because all you need is an email address.

- Don't be picky about the surveys you complete. Again, most of these surveys are limited. If you don't accept a survey immediately, someone else will.

Frequently Asked Questions and Answers

- What is an internet survey?
  - These are surveys mostly conducted by brands for market research or product testing.

- How does online surveys work?
  - Brands usually hire survey companies to conduct the surveys. The company then outsources the completion of the surveys to online contractors.

- How do I earn money from online surveys?
  - You simply sign up with a survey company and complete the surveys that are presented to you.

- How much can I earn from a survey?

- It depends on the scope and nature of the survey. Some surveys pay a few pennies. Some can pay up to $100.

- What are the best survey companies out there?
  - Some of the most popular survey sites today include Swagbucks, Toluna, MySurvey, YouGov, Panel Opinion, and Hiving.

- How do I know if a survey site is legit?
  - Consider how long the site has been around. Fake survey sites don't survive that long. Also read as many reviews as you can about the site.

- What are the requirements in joining a survey site?
  - The requirements vary from one company to another.

- How do I get paid for completed surveys?
  - Most of the time, you will be paid in cash usually through PayPal. Other times, you will be compensated through rewards, coupons, discounts, etc.

- Can I earn a full time income answering surveys?
  - It's possible but it's extremely rare. You should only treat it as source of side income.

- Can I join several survey sites simultaneously?
  - Yes, of course. They are independent from each other so you can join and answer surveys from all of them.

Myth Busters About Online Surveys

- That online surveys always ask dozens of questions at a time. It's not always the case. Some do but not all.

- That majority of online surveys are scams. Sure, some of them are scams but not the majority. You just need to do your due diligence. Read reviews regarding the surveys, check forums for other people's experiences when completing the surveys etc. Fake sites don't tend to stick around for long.

- That online surveys are only meant to steal your information and identity. That's not the case. More often than not, online survey companies run these surveys to better understand how consumers use their products and the features they desire etc. This research information allows them to come up with better products.

- That brands are wasting their time and money in sponsoring surveys. Like I mentioned in 3 above, this is not always a waste of time. It has its use case when executed properly.

- That paid survey sites only hire experienced participants. That's not the case. Anybody can participate in these surveys (you probably need to be above the age of 18)

- That you can easily cheat the system. While this is possible, it's getting harder to pull it off as online survey companies are getting smarter. Inconsistent answers may get you disqualified and you won't get paid.

- That paid surveys are an overnight get-rich-quick scheme. On the contrary, its difficult to make a full time living doing this, much less getting rich quickly!

- That you can get rich by participating in just one paid survey site. This is definitely not feasible.

- That you can simply guess the answers in order to finish them faster and answer more surveys. Like I said before, too many inconsistencies in your answers can get you disqualified.

- That you can make thousands of dollars a month answering a few surveys each week. While this is possible, it's rare. You need to complete a LOT of surveys to possibly make thousand per month.

Inspiration #13

"Success seems to be connected with action. Successful people keep moving. They make mistakes, but they don't quit."

Conrad Hilton

Series #	Book Title
1	Affiliate Marketing
2	Passive Income Ideas
3	Affiliate Marketing + Passive Income Ideas (2-in-1 Bundle)
4	Facebook Advertising
5	Dropshipping
6	Dropshipping + Facebook Advertising (2-in-1 Bundle)
7	Real Estate Investing For Beginners
8	Credit Cards and Credit Repair Secrets
9	Real Estate Investing And Credit Repair Strategies (2-in-1 Bundle)
10	Passive Income Ideas With Affiliate Marketing (2nd Edition)
11	Passive Income With Dividend Investing
12	Stock Market Investing For Beginners
13	The Simple Stock Market Investing Blueprint (2-in-1 Bundle)
14	Real Estate And Stock Market Investing Mastery (3-in-1 Bundle)
15	Amazon FBA Mastery

Business #13

Online Auctions

Online auctions operate exactly like what you'd expect. You list a product in an auction site, set an auction period, set the minimum bid, and then click launch. Customers will bid on your product listing until the auction period ends. Whoever bid the highest after the auction period expired will get your product. This can be a lucrative online business if you are able to target a niche and build an army of loyal customers.

Online auctions require a little bit of work because you need to regularly check which of your auctions have expired and which auctions are still running. Products that didn't get any bids have to be manually relisted. So yes, running an auction business can be time-consuming. But it's worth it if you have products that are easy to sell.

Ratings Based on Our Criteria

A. **Simplicity:**
   The business model of online auction sites is quite simple. Just sign up, list a product, and let potential buyers bid on it.

   8/10

B. **Passivity:**
   You are directly selling products to customers so most of your income isn't passive. Of course, to make it more passive, you can document your processes and hire virtual assistants to help you perform these tasks e.g. listing your items, monitoring bids, relisting unsold items after auction period ends etc.

   5/10

C. **Scalability:**
   To scale the business, you simply add more products in your inventory.

   8/10

D. **Competitiveness:**
   Online auctions are very competitive. Be ready to match other sellers when it comes to prices and quality of products.

   2/10

Tips For Success

- Price your items by reviewing similar products in the auction site that you are using.

- As much as possible, try to offer free shipping. You can double or even triple your customer base with this strategy.

- Learn of the best time in posting your listings. Some products tend to sell better when they are listed within a particular time of the day.

- Always treat your customers properly. Selling in auctions also involves making your customers happy so they'll buy from you again in the future.

- Treat the whole operation like a business. Even if you are not doing it full time.

- If possible, avoid putting reserve prices on your products. Auction customers tend to look for great discounts on items. If they feel there's a limit to the bidding process, it may discourage them from participating.

- Make use of high quality images of your products. It'll make you look more professional and your listings will attract more bids.

- Cross-promote your product listings. If your listings are closely related then this could be a very profitable strategy to implement.

- Offer a return policy. This removes a lot customer fear and barrier to purchase and you can subsequently attract several loyal customers.

- Ask your customers to provide feedback or reviews.

Frequently Asked Questions and Answers

- What is an online auction?
  - An online auction occurs when you list a product for sale and enable customers to bid on it.

- What are the best auction sites today?
  - eBay is without a doubt the largest online auction site today but there are smaller alternatives like Listia, Ubid, Webstore, eCrater, and Bonanza.

- What kind of products can I sell in auction sites?
  - Before you list a product in an auction site, make sure to thoroughly read the terms and agreements and look for the section where the prohibited products are listed.

- How do I collect payments from successful bidders?
  - Auction sites make use of various payment methods. However, the most common methods are through credit card and PayPal.

- How do I cross-promote by product listings?
  - In the description box for a product listing or in the recommendation box, you should feature and highlight your other product listings.

- Is free shipping a good idea?
  - It's a great strategy because it attracts more customers. However, make sure that you aren't at the losing end when you offer free shipping for your products.

- How should I price my products?
  - There are several factors you should consider. These include the cost of the product, the shipping fees, and the charges collected by the auction site.

- What is a reserve price in an online auction?
  - A reserve price is a hidden minimum price that a seller is willing to accept for a product.

- Where can I get products to sell in auction sites?
  - Selling in auction sites is basically a form of retail arbitrage. That is you purchase products from retailers like Target or Walmart and other sources then resell them in an auction site lie eBay.

- How do I promote my product listings in auction sites?
  - Use standard online marketing methods like search engine optimization, social media marketing, advertising, etc.

Myth Busters About Selling in Auction Sites

- That you can't sell products at a fair market value. The word "fair" is subjective. When you list a very valuable product it'll attract a lot of bids and consequently the sale price or "fair price" will be very high. The reverse is the case for poor quality products.

- That selling products using an auction site can be very expensive and inflate the prices of products. It is not unusual for auction sites to take a cut of the revenue made from selling your product. However, it need not be expensive. You can mark-up your product to account for this additional fee.

- That auctions only attract buyers who are looking for a bargain. This may be true at times. However, it's not always the case. You get the occasional customers who appreciate the value of what you're offering and are willing to bid accordingly

- That it's very difficult to find good deals in auction sites. If you look hard enough you'll always find good deals.

- That auction sites are rigged by both the sellers and owners of the site. This is not true. Rigging or Shill bidding is against most website owners terms of service e.g. Ebays would ban you if you're caught in violation of their TOS. That being said, some sellers do engage in shill bidding.

- That online auctions serve as a last resort for both buyers and sellers. There are other sites where buyers and sellers can transact e.g. Amazon

- That most of the products being sold in auction sites are either pre-owned or of lower quality. This is not true. You can purchase brand new items from ebay.

- That auction sites are swindling sellers and buyers with hidden costs and fees. Some are but not all of them. Do your due diligence and understand which features are free and which aren't. Research the auction sites, check their reviews on other independent sites, read forum comments and see what sellers are saying about the auction site. Are they mostly positive or negative etc.

- That you can't make real money selling in auction sites. You can if you know what you're doing with regards to pricing, finding products at a great discount so you have enough margin for profit when you resell, great list photos and optimized sales pages highlighting the product features/benefits etc.

- That auction sites are taking most of the profits you make from your sales. They don't take the majority of your money. However, it's not uncommon for auction sites to take about 10-15% of your revenue in fees.

Inspiration #14

"If you really want to do something, you'll find a way. If you don't, you'll find an excuse."
Jim Rohn

Business #14

Cryptocurrency

If you haven't heard about cryptocurrencies, then you have probably been living under a rock for the last decade or so. Just kidding. Cryptocurrencies have taken the online economy by storm. Just a few years ago Bitcoin, the very first digital currency, was introduced to the world. Today, a single Bitcoin is worth more than $6000. Bitcoin was a huge success that other digital currencies like Litecoin and Ethereum were able to rise in value and influence. Now, you can generate a nice income by trading and investing in digital coins.

There are three main ways on how you can make money from cryptocurrencies. One, buy and trade them. There are several cryptocurrency exchanges out there that can facilitate such transactions. Two, you accept cryptocurrencies as payment for specific products and services. And three, you mine your own cryptocurrencies. If you are new in the industry, I suggest that you follow option 1 or 2 or both. Option 3 is just too difficult and/or expensive to pull off these days.

Ratings Based on Our Criteria

A. **Simplicity:**
   Trying to make money from cryptocurrencies if far from being simple. You need to spend time educating yourself on the latest revolution and the intricacies of how they work.
   4/10
B. **Passivity:**
   You can make passive income from your Cryptocurrency by lending it to people who will pay you interest on them. There are B2B lending platforms that specialize in helping you lend your Bitcoin e.g. Bitbond, BTCPOP, KIVA etc.
   7/10
C. **Scalability:**
   To scale up your earnings, you have to purchase more coins and repeat the steps discussed above.
   6/10
D. **Competitiveness:**
   The cryptocurrency industry is already competitive. Expect it to get even more competitive in the coming years as more people warm up to it.
   3/10

Tips For Success

- Learn everything you can about the industry before you jump into the bandwagon.
- Do your research and determine the differences between popular cryptocurrencies like Bitcoin, Litecoin, and Ethereum.
- Trade only amounts you can afford to lose and only when you have a clear strategy.
- For each trade, you must set a clear target level for taking profit and more importantly, a stop-loss level for decreasing losses.
- Always consider the risks and don't be greedy. Look for the smaller profits that can accumulate into bigger profits down the road.
- Be aware of the fees that are associated with multiple trade actions.
- Don't go looking for crashed coins expecting them to rise in value again.
- Don't put all of your eggs in one basket. Invest in at least two cryptocurrencies.
- Only use cryptocurrency exchanges that have proven themselves to be secure and reliable.
- Use an exchange, not a broker. You'll save a lot of money and time this way.

Frequently Asked Questions and Answers

- What is a cryptocurrency?
    - It's a virtual exchange medium that utilizes cryptography to secure transactions and control the creation of the currencies.

- Why use cryptocurrency?
    - Cryptocurrencies are well-known for their anonymity and security.

- How many types of cryptocurrencies are out there today?
    - Estimates show that there are over 900 cryptocurrencies today, most of which are obscure and operate under extreme secrecy.

- What are the biggest cryptocurrencies that I should invest on?
    - The most widely used digital currencies today are Bitcoin, Ethereum, Litecoin, Zcash, Dash, Ripple, and Monero.

- How difficult is it to obtain a digital coin?
    - It depends on several factors. But there are basically three ways on how to get one. Purchase it, accept it as payment for goods or services, or mine it.

- What is cryptocurrency mining?
    - This is a process in which transactions for various forms of cryptocurrency are verified and added to the blockchain digital ledger.

- What is a cryptocurrency wallet?
    - This is a secure digital wallet used to store, send, and receive digital currency like Bitcoin.

- When is the right time to sell a digital coin?
    - There's no universally accepted "best time" to sell your cryptocurrency. Suffice it to say, this will depend on your investment strategy i.e. are you investing for the long term or are you a short term trader looking to profit off of temporary fluctuations in cryptocurrency prices. Be that as it may, you may want to consider selling your coin when its value is 25% more than that of when you purchased it.

- How risky is cryptocurrency trading?
    - Just think of the risks associated with the stock market. The cryptocurrency market is subjected to similar fluctuations and risks.

- Can I transfer cryptocurrencies across countries?
    - Yes, that's the beauty of digital currencies. They are decentralized.

Myth Busters about Trading Cryptocurrencies

- That cryptocurrencies are being used by criminals to avoid the law and taxes. With Bitcoin, every single transaction is public, which is not exactly ideal if you are looking to engage in illegal activities.

- That it's easy to buy and sell digital coins. It's one thing buying and selling digital coins and another thing doing it profitably. To do the later, education is very important.

- That cryptocurrencies have no real value at all because they aren't backed by anything. The intrinsic value of Bitcoin partly lies in the ability to mine it. It's infrastructure is intentionally set up to reward miners: if more miners attempt to create Bitcoin then it automatically becomes more difficult to profit from the process. Likewise, if fewer miners make the attempt, then it becomes easier to make money this way. A Bitcoin's intrinsic value, therefore, is in the representation of the effort it takes to mine it.

- That cryptocurrencies always prioritize anonymity.

- That it's illegal to trade and deal in cryptocurrencies. The legal status of Bitcoin varies substantially from country to country and is still undefined or changing in many of them. Whereas the majority of countries do not make the usage of Bitcoin itself illegal, its status as money varies, with differing regulatory implications.

- That cryptocurrencies are mere fads that will soon go away. According to investor James Altucher, cryptocurrencies like Bitcoin are here to stay. Mainstream banks will accept Bitcoin, and will start offering storage and software access. They will also create cryptocurrency derivatives – as the CME is about to start doing. Despite the optimism, there will be a massive wipeout, and 95 percent of the alt-coins out there will go away – just like the dot-com bust.

- That cryptocurrencies are only for tech-savvy hackers. Anyone can invest in cryptocurrency if they're willing to educate themselves or, at the very least, partner with people who know what they're doing

- That bitcoins are associated and connected to organized crime. This is not entirely true. Criminals understand that Bitcoin's blockchain technology can work against them. This is because the digital ledger meticulously records which addresses send and receive transactions, including the exact time and amount – great data to use as evidence.

- That cryptocurrencies can't be used to purchase real goods and services. This is not true. As cryptocurrencies continue to go mainstream, more and more businesses are accepting it as a means of payment for real goods and services.

- That cryptocurrencies are all the same. This is not true. Ethereum is backed by a blockchain, much like Bitcoin, but the technology is slightly different and aimed at a specific use case: smart contracts.

Congratulations!

The fourth character of the password required to unlock the business scorecard is letter c.

Inspiration #15

"I cannot give you the formula for success, but I can give you the formula for failure--It is: Try to please everybody."

Herbert Bayard Swope

Business #15

Commodities Trading

Commodities trading can be an effective way to diversify your portfolio. It doesn't matter if you are in it for the short term or for the long haul. Always keep in mind that a commodity market is a market that trades in primary economic sectors rather than manufactured products. Tradable commodities include metals, energy, livestock and meat, and other agricultural products. Commodities trading has a lot of similarities with stock trading. The biggest difference lies in the assets that are being traded. Commodity trading focuses on buying and trading commodities like gold and other precious metals instead of company shares as in stock trading.

However, you should take note that there's a process you need to follow to become a commodities trader. This process varies per country. For example, in the United States, in order to become a licensed commodity trader, you need to register and get licensed by the National Futures Association or NFA. It's advisable that you get in touch with the proper agencies on how you should proceed.

Ratings Based on Our Criteria

A. **Simplicity:**
To be a successful commodities trader, you need to be ahead of the curve and smart (i.e. have the ability to see the big picture, make sense of macro and micro economic events, policies, regulations etc. and, more importantly, understand how the market will react to them and how to position yourself to profit from such market moves)

6/10

B. **Passivity:**
Just like in the stock market, a lot of the income you make from commodities trading are passive income. You analyze the situation, establish your position, set your stop loss and wait.

7/10

C. **Scalability:**
To scale the business, you have to invest in more commodities and/or trade on margin. Note that trading on margin can be very risky but it'll give you more leverage (especially if you know what you're doing).

7/10

D. **Competitiveness:**
The commodities market is very competitive. You have to compete against both small businessmen and huge corporations (investment banks etc.).

3/10

Tips For Success

- Seek the help of an expert or a financial consultant before you jump on the bandwagon.
- Adopt a definite investing plan.
- Don't trade in too many markets. Chances are your investment strategy will work exceptionally well in either bull or bear markets but not both. Understand when to take action and when to sit on the fence.
- Don't trade in a market that is too thin i.e. not enough liquidity. These tend to be highly volatile and if you do not have the emotional maturity to tolerate such fluctuations, you may not follow through with your investment strategy.

- Always start with your own investment and financial goals. Make sure you know how a financial product helps you advance towards your goals.
- Don't chase a hot tip. When you make an investment, its important you know the reasons for doing it
- Sell the losers and let the winners ride
- Never ever overtrade because you might lose all of your capital.
- Unless you know what you're doing, never add to a losing position because if the position continues to go against you, your account will suffer huge losses especially if you are trading on margin.
- Focus on the future. The tough part about investing is that we are trying to make informed decisions based on things that have yet to happen. It's important to keep in mind that even though we use past data as an indication of things to come, its what happens in the future that matters most.

Frequently Asked Questions and Answers

- What does it mean to trade in commodities?
  - To trade commodities involves watching the commodity market and then taking positions based on forecasted trends or arbitrage opportunities.

- What are the most common commodities being traded?
  - The most commonly traded commodities are crude oil, natural gas, heating oil, sugar, gold, corn, wheat, soybeans, copper, and cotton.

- How do commodities markets work?
  - The commodities market works just like most markets. It's a physical or virtual marketplace where one can purchase, sell, or trade various commodities.

- How do I invest in the commodity market?
  - You can do it by investing in commodity-related stocks or you can trade the commodities yourself.

- How much money does a commodity trader make?
  - It depends on your experience. Traders with less than three years of experience usually have an average base salary of $100,000 to $150,000.

- How do I get licensed as a commodities trader?
  - It depends on your location and country. Get in touch with the proper agency for further advice.

- Can I trade commodities online?
  - Yes, many online trading platforms allow you to do so.

- Where can I trade commodities online?
  - Some of the more reputable online trading platforms today include TD Ameritrade, TradeStation, Generic Trade, MB, and Lightspeed.

- Is it safe to trade commodities online?
  - It's safe as long as you only deal with reliable brokers, companies, and trading platforms.

- How huge are the risks in trading commodities?
  - Commodities trading is often riskier than stock trading. Always keep that in mind.

Myth Busters about Trading Commodities

- That commodities trading is for speculators only. Speculators are an important link in the market. However, they work only because someone on the other side of the trade is hedging their risk. These market participants could be hedgers, arbitrageurs etc. They help in efficient price discovery and price-risk management.

- That understanding the commodities is too difficult for ordinary people. All commodities are globally traded and the demand supply dynamics are widely known and available to the public. So, understanding commodities trading is not complex as long as you're willing to learn.

- That there is no assurance on quality of commodities delivered. Most exchanges have quality control measures in place to ensure that commodities delivered to their warehouses meet high quality standards.

- That commodity markets are too volatile. Commodities are no more volatile than stocks if the leverage is removed. Unlike stocks, which can move up to 20 percent in a single session, metal and energy contracts can rise or fall up to 6% in a single day.

- That commodity markets and exchanges provide fire for inflation.

- That it's too difficult to earn money through commodities trading. This happens only when market participants do not trade with discipline and fall victim to greed and fear.

- That commodity trading is only for high net-worth investors and large traders. This is not true. Like any other derivatives market, anybody can trade by paying a small percentage of the total value of the contract.

- That the delivery of commodities is compulsory. There is compulsory delivery in commodities such as gold. However, an investor cannot take delivery of crude oil and metals, as trade in these two commodities are cash settled.

- That prices in the commodities market are too easy to manipulate and rig. Most commodities that are traded are produced and consumed across the globe. As such, any person or group of persons cannot easily manipulate prices.

- That you need a lot of money to get started trading commodities. This is not true as you can wield tremendous leverage trading on margin with little capital.

Inspiration #16

"If you dream it, you can do it."

Walt Disney

Business #16

Make YouTube Videos

YouTube can be a great source of passive income if you have a unique voice and unique content that gets a following on the video-sharing website. Money you earn from your YouTube content is passive income because the videos will keep on earning as long as they are up on the site. There are three major ways on how you can monetize your YouTube videos. One, you sign up with Google Adsense. Two, you directly promote a product or a service on your videos. And three, you promote products in the descriptions of your videos. You can use all three monetization strategies if you want.

Setting up a YouTube channel is free and easy. But if you want to turn it into a source of passive income, you have to approach it like a business. This means you need to do your research and decide on the kind of topics and material that you are going to cover in your channel. You also need to decide what genre your channel will be in. Will you be doing commentary videos, unboxing videos, comedy skits, science videos, tutorials, etc.?

You also need to build your audience first before you monetize your videos. This is going to take some time so you should have long-term goals. Don't expect people to be flocking to your channel after several videos. Sometimes, it takes dozens of good videos to finally get their attention.

Ratings Based on Our Criteria

A. **Simplicity:**
Shooting and editing videos require a lot of time and a lot of work. This is especially true if you are not that skilled when it comes to video editing. It gets easier with time but maintaining the quality of your videos still requires effort. That being said, the editing process can be outsourced to freelancers who are good at them. This will free up time for you to do what you do best – record quality videos!

6/10

B. **Passivity:**
If you have an archive of videos, you can earn a good amount of passive income from them. What's especially good about this business model is that videos you filmed and uploaded months or years ago will continue to earn you passive income as long as the ads stay active.

9/10

C. **Scalability:**
You can scale your passive earnings from your videos by creating not only higher-quality content but also more videos. The math is simple. If you double your output without compromising the quality, you can potentially double your earnings. Furthermore, the world is your oyster as there's no limit to how many people can view your videos and how much you can earn.

9/10

D. **Competitiveness:**
Competition depends on your niche but whatever niche you are in there are probably dozens of other YouTubers talking about the same topics as you.

4/10

Tips For Success

- Focus on a niche. If you are going to look into the most successful channels on YouTube, most of them are focusing on a specific niche. If you are going to talk about movies, then 99% of your content should be about movies.

- Make your titles, tags, and descriptions clear and direct to the point. This is one way of getting your videos found within the platform. With the right titles and tags, your video will appear as a recommended video alongside other videos that have the same or similar themes and topics as yours.

- Use analytics to understand how viewers interact with your videos. YouTube has its own in-built analytics tool that you can use. There you can see where your viewers are coming from, how they are commenting, and which sections of your channel are getting the most attention. Essentially, you figure out what works best and double down on it.

- Share links to your content in other platforms like Facebook, Twitter, Instagram, and Pinterest. The more you share your videos, the more views you get.

- Post teasers of your YouTube videos in other video-sharing websites like Vimeo and Facebook. For example, you can cut a 1-minute video from the full video and post it on Facebook. People who enjoyed the video will want more so they end up watching the full video in your YouTube channel.

- Create an eye-catching thumbnail for your videos. This is a powerful technique because a lot of viewers often pre-judge a video's content by looking at the thumbnail. Eye-catching thumbnails translate to more views for your videos.

- Collaborate with other YouTube creators in your niche. For example, if you are doing movie reviews, you can collaborate with another movie reviewer to create a double feature review. You leverage each other's influence to build your subscriber list.

- Try doing live videos on YouTube. The platform has a livestream feature which is a good way to build relationships with your most avid viewers.

- Develop video series. This is similar to creating a book series. You nurture interest in your content by creating a series wherein your viewers can't help but look forward to the next installment.

- Commit to a schedule when posting videos. This way, your viewers will know when the next video will be uploaded. If weeks go by without a new video, people will starts unsubscribing.

Frequently Asked Questions and Answers

- How exactly do I monetize a YouTube video?
  - There are several ways but the three most common monetization methods are as follows. One, you sign up with Google Adsense and activate it in your videos. Two, you promote affiliate products in the description box of your videos. And three, attract brands and businesses that might be willing to sponsor your videos.

- What is Google Adsense?
  - At least 70% of the people earning money from their YouTube videos earn it through Google Adsense. Google owns both Adsense and YouTube. Adsense delivers the ads that are shown inside and alongside your videos on YouTube. To make money from Adsense, you have to submit an application

first. Once you are approved, you connect your Adsense account with your YouTube account. You then activate ads in your videos. That's it.

- What is vlogging?
  - The term is a shortened version of the phrase "video blogging". The term became very popular with the rise of video bloggers using YouTube. Instead of writing down your content in the case of blogging, you create a video log.

- How do I sell merchandise like affiliate products on YouTube?
  - There are two major ways on how you can do this. One, you simply talk about a product in one of your videos either in the form of a review or as a recommended product in relation to the topic of the video. You then place in the video's description box a link to where viewers can purchase the product. Two, you can place a link back to your own store in the description of every video you make.

- How do I get more subscribers on YouTube?
  - Your success as a YouTube content creator or vlogger is often measured by how much subscribers you have. With that said, you should spend a considerable amount of your time and resources in attracting new subscribers. The quality of your content is still your most important tool in getting subscribers. Aside from creating great content, you should also make use of well-known strategies like instructing viewers to subscribe at the end of every video, running contests, and buying ads within YouTube.

- How do I get my videos to be added in the recommendation bar in YouTube?
  - If you watch a video on YouTube, you can see a list of recommended videos on the right side of your screen. This is a feature that you can exploit to get more views for your own videos. So how do you do it? Well, it's just a matter of using the right titles, tags, and descriptions for your videos. Let's say you have a video about hiking in Alaska. You should make use of clear titles and tags like "hiking", "Alaska", "mountain climbing", "trekking", "adventure", or "nature" if you want your video to be recommended in the side bar of videos that contain the same themes and topics.

- Why am I getting a copyright strike on my videos?
  - This is a question that a lot of newbies ask because they are unfamiliar with YouTube's content policies. Generally speaking, you can't use licensed and copyrighted materials in your videos. If you do, you will likely receive a copyright strike. If you get numerous strikes, YouTube can easily and suddenly terminate your account. With that said, avoid using video clips, images, and music that you don't own or don't have any right of using.

- What is the YouTube Partner Program?
  - This is the advertising program by Google that allows vloggers and content creators in YouTube to earn money from their videos. It enables creators to have ads served on their videos. Before you can be in the program, you have to apply first through your account in the Creator Studio.

- What are the requirements of the YouTube Partner Program?
  - In early 2018, YouTube has changed the requirements for eligibility in the YouTube Partner Program. For your channel to be eligible, you should have at least 1,000 subscribers and 4,000 hours of watch time within the past twelve (12) months. YouTube explained that these new rules serve as protection against spammers, impersonators, content thieves, and other bad actors who are ruining YouTube's ecosystem.

- If I get a strike on a video, is there a way to fix it and make the video monetizable again?

- Yes, you can always appeal if you receive a strike for a video you uploaded. However, your video wouldn't be reinstated if it's clear that you violated any of YouTube's policies and rules. Your appeal can only be reviewed if none of your content made use of licensed and copyrighted materials.

Myth Busters About Making Money on YouTube

- That you don't need expertise to attract a following. You don't need to be an expert per se. However, you need to be knowledgeable about something – something you can share with the world, have your own opinion on and add your own unique spin on things.

- That you can earn hundreds of dollars in your first month. Consistently coming up with quality content and growing a following takes time. This is by no means a get rich quick scheme!

- That monetizing your videos is easy. Not necessarily, you still need to come up with quality content that'll attract and keep viewers subscribed. You also need to comply with YouTube's terms and conditions

- That attracting sponsors for your videos is easy. It's only easy if you have a strong bargaining chip i.e. a good following and quality content on your YouTube channel. When you have these in place, businesses will be eager to partner with you.

- That success in other social media sites like Facebook and Instagram can translate to instant success in YouTube. That's not always the case. Some of these platforms appeal to different demographics and people there consume information in a different way.

- That product review videos are a thing of the past. On the contrary, these are still going strong. People are always looking to learn more about items they're considering purchasing and most prefer to consume this information via video instead of articles.

- That unboxing videos are no longer popular. Like product review videos above, these are still popular.

- That more views equal to more revenue. This isn't always the case.

- That you can upload a video and watch the revenue roll in. It takes time and consistency to build a following. Once that is in place, you'll begin to see your income grow.

- That YouTube will shut down sponsored videos in the future. This is doubtful as YouTube, much like Facebook, rely on revenue from ads. Unless they figure out a more profitable way to monetize their platform, sponsored videos aren't going anywhere.

Inspiration #17

"A successful man is one who can lay a firm foundation with the bricks that other throw at him."
David Brinkley

Business #17

Social Media Influencer

What is a social media influencer? Think of the Kardashian sisters. Whether you like them or not, they are the very epitome of social media influencers. They have millions of followers in social networking sites like Facebook, Instagram, Twitter, and Snapchat. To be a social media influencer, you must have a sizable following in social media. It doesn't have to be as big as the Kardashians but it should be enough to get the attention of businesses and brands. Your following should be enough to the point that businesses and brands approach you to promote or review a certain product or service.

As a social media influencer, your main source of income will be from businesses and brands that get you to promote and talk about a product. But that's not the only monetization model that you can use. If you have thousands of followers, you can always direct them to another digital asset like a blog where you promote and sell products and services. That's how other social media influencers monetize their following. You can follow the same business model.

For example, let's say that you run a Facebook page with thousands of followers. In the page, you talk about and review beauty products. To earn passive income from your influence, you can tie up a blog with your Facebook page. In the blog, you have more content about the beauty products that you have featured on your Facebook page. Your avid followers and fans will visit your blog with the right promotion. In the blog, you can earn money by promoting affiliate products or by displaying advertisements that are relevant to beauty and makeup.

Ratings Based on Our Criteria

A. **Simplicity:**
   Being a social media influencer takes a lot of time and work. You have to spend time running and managing your social media profiles every single day. If you slow down, you run the risk of losing some of your influence. Like most other business models, this can be simplified by outsourcing the management of these social media accounts to virtual assistants.

   8/10

B. **Passivity:**
   This business model is not entirely passive. As I mentioned above, it takes a lot of time and work. Yes, some of your earnings are passive in nature (e.g. earnings from affiliate products, podcasts, webinars, retainer fee from being a brand ambassador etc.) but others earning avenues aren't (e.g. hosting events, doing store appearances, product reviews etc.). How passive this is for you will depend on which avenue you leverage the most and how successful you are at outsourcing those tasks that aren't so important e.g. managing your social media account, editing your videos etc.

   7/10

C. **Scalability:**
   The only way to scale your earnings in this business is to increase your influence. That means you have to attract more likes, more followers, more subscribers, and more loyal fans. Networking and collaborating with other influencers can also help you achieve this.

   6/10

D. **Competitiveness:**
   It can be difficult to maintain your influence on a social media platform given the fact that there are probably thousands of other people trying to get to where you are.

   3/10

Tips For Success

- Find your focus. In order to transform yourself into an influencer, you must be a master in a specific topic or niche. In short, please don't cast your net too wide.

- Subscribe to other platforms blogs so that you are in the loop when changes are implemented. For example, what if Instagram introduces a new feature? If you are not in the loop, it will probably be too late before you start using the new feature.

- Set alerts for topics and keywords in your niche. As a social media influencer, your followers expect you to be updated about the latest happenings in your niche. You can use Google Alerts to track the latest developments in your niche.

- Write a blog and tie it up with your social media accounts. If you are popular in Instagram, that doesn't mean it's unnecessary for you to start a blog. In fact, you can direct more potential followers to your Instagram account through your blog.

- Get on LinkedIn. Many people dismiss LinkedIn but it can be a very powerful tool to connect you with the right people at the right time. It's a great place to find business partners and collaborators.

- Engage with your fans and followers whenever you can. Try to reply to as many comments and messages as you can. A single reply can make the difference between a disgruntled fan and a lifelong fan.

- Always keep it real. It's getting easier to spot bullshit on the internet so don't ever think of lying to or misleading your followers. One lie can ruin everything that you've worked for.

- Collaborate with other social media influencers. Popular online celebrities do this all the time and after every collaboration, there's always a significant boost in their subscribers and fans.

- Have a sense of humor. Funny sells. That's a fact. Again, if you look into the most popular social media influencers online, majority of them are popular because they are funny. If you can make a person laugh, that person can be easily converted into an avid fan.

- Run contests and giveaways. This is a tried and tested method of getting a boost in attention. Not only is this a powerful way of engaging with your established fans, it's also a powerful way to attract new fans.

Frequently Asked Questions and Answers

- What is a social media influencer?
  - A social media influencer is someone who has a following on a social media platform.

- What is influencer marketing?
  - This is the practice of hiring online influencers to promote products and services to their followers and fans.

- How do social media influencers make money?
  - There are several ways. They can be paid by sponsors. They can earn money from their own blogs and websites. Sometimes, fans can even pay them directly e.g. via Patreon.

- What's the difference between an influencer and a brand ambassador?
  - The two are very similar. The biggest differences lie in the kind of work they do and how they are compensated.

- How do I qualify as a social media influencer?
  - There are no written rules on what separates an influencer from the rest. All you need is a good following online. You are an influencer if there are people following you and your every move.

- Which social media sites are the best platforms for social media influencers?
  - So far, the most popular influencers are concentrated in just a few platforms which include Facebook, Instagram, YouTube, and Twitter.

- How do I reach out to brands who might want to partner with me as an influencer?
  - Just directly contact them and present your sales pitch. Show them why your following is good for their business. You can either contact the directly via their website, email or LinkedIn.

- How much should you charge for your services as an influencer?
  - It depends on various metrics and factors. How many people are following you? How lucrative is your niche? What's your main demographic? Etc.

- Can you make a full-time income from being a social media influencer alone?
  - It's definitely possible.

- How do I get paid as a social media influencer?
  - You can choose to be paid in cash or with rewards. It depends on your deals with brands and sponsors.

Myth Busters about Being a Social Media Influencer

- That it's easy to become a social media influencer. Nothing worthwhile is easy at first. It takes time to build your own following

- That influencer marketing is only for beautiful and attractive people. That's not true. Anyone can become an influencer. As long as you have something to offer be it your knowledge, your lifestyle etc.

- That you can monetize any social media platform. That may not always be the case. Some are much harder (if at all possible) to monetize e.g. YouTube vs Twitter.

- That if you have a huge following, brands and sponsors will start reaching out to you. While this can happen, it's not always the case. You still need to reach out to them. Let them know who you are and what you can offer them.

- That you don't need to spend money to become a social media influencer. You will need to spend money creating content, running ads to your website, YouTube and Facebook page etc.

- That working with social media personalities is unprofessional. There's nothing unprofessional about working with social media influencers. They are a trusted voice and they help create content, build brand awareness, generate sales etc. Partnering up with them is a no brainer.

- That the effectiveness of influencer marketing can't be tracked and measured.

- That influencers will only work with brands if they are compensated in cash. There are other creative ways influencers may want to be compensated e.g. Invitation to events, exclusive access to brand updates and products, all-expenses-paid trips etc.

- That an influencer's total reach and social follower numbers are more important than audience engagement and relevance. Engagement and relevance are more important. Otherwise, you'll lose a lot of subscribers who feel your content isn't consistent enough or relevant to them.

- That short-form social content yields the same value as long-form content. It's not that clear cut as this can be platform specific e.g. people on Instagram or Facebook don't expect to consume hour-long videos. However, on YouTube they won't mind.

Inspiration #18

"Many of life's failures are people who did not realize how close they were to success when they gave up."
Thomas Edison

Business #18

Photography – Royalty from Photographs

If you have photography skills, you can earn from your photographs by listing them in stock photography sites. In the simplest of terms, stock photography sites are e-commerce platforms where you can upload high-resolution copies of your photos and have people use them for a fee. For example, let's say that a nature magazine like National Geographic wants to use a wilderness photo you uploaded in a stock photography website. For a fee, the magazine can use your photograph one time (or several times) depending on the terms of agreement. You earn a royalty from the transaction.

You still own the photograph so other magazines, newspapers, online media outlets, businesses, and individuals can use it. You earn a royalty every time a customer downloads and uses your photo. There are numerous stock photography websites out there that you can use. These include Fotolia, Overstock, and ShutterStock. Try signing up with these stock companies and test out their services. Some stock companies are good for certain types of photographs so you should take the time to experiment with them.

Ratings Based on Our Criteria

A. **Simplicity:**
Earning passive income from stock photographs is simple in the sense that the barriers to entry are low. All you have to do is sign up with stock photography companies and upload your best photos.
9/10

B. **Passivity:**
As long as a photo of yours is uploaded in a stock photography website, it has the potential to earn you royalties in perpetuity. It doesn't get anymore passive than that!
10/10

C. **Scalability:**
To scale your earnings from stock photography, you simply increase the quality and number of photos you upload.
9/10

D. **Competitiveness:**
Unfortunately, given the low barrier to entry, the competition in stock photography is really tough. Pretty much anyone with a camera can become a photographer. Even with just a smartphone, you can take high-quality photos and upload them in stock photography sites.
3/10

Tips For Success

- License and copyright your photos before you upload them in stock photography websites and agencies. Theft is very rampant in the photography industry. You can't make money from your photos if someone steals it and claims it as his or her own.

- Focus your attention and efforts on the most reputable stock photography sites. These are Shutterstock, Dreamstime, Fotolia, iStockphoto, and Freedigitalphotos. These have the biggest clientele and marketplace so you have a much better chance of getting sales from them.

- Create a portfolio of your best photos. You can show off this portfolio in your website, blog, Facebook page, or Instagram page.

- Submit only your best and most interesting photos. Always keep in mind that if you upload a photo, there's probably hundreds of photos that are similar to it. So make sure that your photo is unique before you hit on the upload button.

- Keep it simple. Stock photography is not high art. Most of the people and companies looking for photos in stock photography sites are looking for something clear and simple.

- Don't over-retouch your photos. It's so much easier to spot retouched photos these days. There are even programs and apps that can easily identify retouched photos from the un-retouched ones.

- Look for a niche and master it. There are hundreds of thousands of professional photographers out there trying to make their mark in stock photography. Needless to say, the competition is very tough. You can make your life easier by finding a niche with less competition and dominating that niche.

- Make use of descriptive titles and tags when naming and describing your photos. Search engine optimization is very important in helping your photos get found online. Think of yourself as a customer. If you are looking for a particular stock photo, what are the words and phrases that you are going to use to search for it?

- Learn how to negotiate. This is very important if you are directly communicating with companies or people who want to purchase some of your stock photos. Don't undersell or oversell your work.

- Invest in high-quality photography gear. If you have better gear, you will be able to shoot better-looking photos. It's as simple as that.

Frequently Asked Questions and Answers

- What are stock photographs?
  - These are licensed and copyrighted photos that clients can use for a one-time fee.

- Do I still own the rights to my photographs?
  - Yes, the photographs are still yours. Clients are merely paying you a fee for the chance to them.

- What are the top stock photography sites?
  - These would be Shutterstock, Fotolia, Dreamstine, Getty Images, and iStock Photo.

- What are the requirements in uploading photos to these sites?
  - It varies per site so you should read their Terms of Agreement well before joining.

- Are my photos safe when I upload them in stock sites?
  - There is always the possibility that some people will steal them and use them without your permission.

- How much can I earn listing my photos in stock sites?
  - It depends on the stock photo agency and their corresponding rates.

- What kind of photos sell best in stock sites?

  - Go for images that have commercial appeal. These are the kinds of images that are usually used in advertising and in the media.

- Can I submit my photos to more than one stock site?
  - Yes, you absolutely can. Remember that you own the rights to your photos.

- What about exclusivity?
  - An exclusivity deal is when you agree to upload your photos in just one stock site. There are obvious benefits to this some of which are earning a higher royalty, higher upload limit, higher ranking in search engines, showcasing your work on the websites homepage etc. However, there are disadvantages too, like the fact you cannot sell it anywhere else (and in many cases not even on your own website), higher selling price of your image (even if your image cannot be purchased anywhere else, will a customer be happy to pay more for it? If its top quality, probably yes. But that's a big if)

- Do I need a model release for photos that feature recognizable people?
  - Yes. All photos containing recognizable faces require a model release.

Myth Busters about Stock Photography

- That you don't need stock photography because you can just Google for images. Unless you're willing to entertain potential legal issues, you'll do well to steer clear of images from Google that aren't labeled for reuse.

- That stock photography is available to everyone so everyone ends up with similar images. If you spend time brainstorming concepts and reviewing your model choices, medium and color schemes, it's highly unlikely you'll have the exact same image as someone else.

- That stock photography is too stocky and cheesy. If you follow current trend, you'll have a better understanding of the type of images that are in high demand and one thing is for sure – they're far from stocky.

- That stock photography is very expensive. This is not always the case. Depositphotos has a flexible plan where images will cost about $1 each.

- That stock photos are all the same and that they rarely change.

- That majority of stock images are done by amateurs.

- That stock images don't always look professional. This is simply not true. The majority of photographers tend to be professional

- That stock photography lacks authenticity. This is not always the case. That being said, Stock photography is always evolving. The majority of photographers understand this movement and are edging closer to more authentic photography

- That stock images are homogenous. No they're not. If you're not finding the images you want, it's a matter of being more specific and creative with keywords.

- That stock images are blatant knock-offs.

Inspiration #19

"Don't be distracted by criticism. Remember--the only taste of success some people get is to take a bite out of you."

Zig Ziglar

Series #	Book Title
1	Affiliate Marketing
2	Passive Income Ideas
3	Affiliate Marketing + Passive Income Ideas (2-in-1 Bundle)
4	Facebook Advertising
5	Dropshipping
6	Dropshipping + Facebook Advertising (2-in-1 Bundle)
7	Real Estate Investing For Beginners
8	Credit Cards and Credit Repair Secrets
9	Real Estate Investing And Credit Repair Strategies (2-in-1 Bundle)
10	Passive Income Ideas With Affiliate Marketing (2nd Edition)
11	Passive Income With Dividend Investing
12	Stock Market Investing For Beginners
13	The Simple Stock Market Investing Blueprint (2-in-1 Bundle)
14	Real Estate And Stock Market Investing Mastery (3-in-1 Bundle)
15	Amazon FBA Mastery

Download The Audio Versions Along With The Complementary PDF Document For FREE from www.MichaelEzeanaka.com

Business #19

Real Estate - REITS

Investing in real estate is one of the purest ways of generating passive income especially if you plan on accumulating property that you then improve and rent out. Rental income is a common example of passive income. What's great about real estate is that you have numerous options on how to invest in it. You can purchase a property, build a structure upon it, and then rent it out.

To take the hassle out of real estate investing and make it even more passive, you can invest in what is referred to as real estate investment trusts or REITs. Basically, a REIT is a firm that owns, operates, and finances a range of income-producing real estate properties. Examples of properties that a REIT may own and operate include office buildings, apartments, warehouses, hospitals, shopping centers, hotels, motels, and even timberlands.

To invest in REITs, you should look for a REIT whose stocks are publicly traded. Get in touch with a reliable broker who will purchase the shares for you. You can also purchase shares from a non-traded REIT through another broker who deals with offerings by non-traded REITs.

Ratings Based on Our Criteria

A. **Simplicity:**
Investing in real estate especially in real estate investment trusts can be very complicated. You need to educate yourself to understand how to analyze REITS and make investment decisions. Working with a mentor can fast track this learning process.

5/10

B. **Passivity:**
What's great about real estate investments is that the vast majority of the earnings you make are passive.

9/10

C. **Scalability:**
To scale your earnings, you just have to invest in more real estate properties.

7/10

D. **Competitiveness:**
Real estate is one of the most competitive industries out there.

3/10

Tips For Success

- Work closely with your accountant to understand the tax implications of REIT investing and how to take advantage of them.

- Know the different types of REITS. While there are some diversified REITS, most specialize in a single property type. Common REIT specialties include: retail, healthcare, industrial, residential, hotel etc.

- Know the right metrics to use when evaluating REITS. The first metric you need to learn is funds from operation or FFO, which is the REITS version of "earnings". This metric adds back in property depreciation and makes a few other adjustments to accurately show a REITS income and, therefore, its ability to pay dividends. There are other important metrics you can learn such as debt coverage, net asset value, intrinsic value etc.

- Understand the risks involved. Interest-rate risk is a big one, as higher interest rates tend to create downward pressure on REIT stock prices.

- Keep and maintain a good credit report. This comes in handy for a lot of your future investments and will save you a lot of money.

- Don't over-leverage yourself. You can be very successful for a long time and still go broke if every rental property is mortgaged to the hilt. Find the right balance and a few longer-than-expected vacancies or dips in your cash flow won't be the end of your career.

- Look for rental properties in emerging neighbourhood. An emerging neighbourhood is a section in a town or city that's attracting moneyed and influential people.

- Diversify your investments. Investing across a large geographical area will also further diversity your investments and protect your portfolio against the volatility of local markets.

- Do not overload your portfolio to chase REIT yields.

- Stick with publicly traded REITs. Non-traded REITs are still good but you have better chances achieving success with their publicly traded counterparts. It's also more appealing in the sense that the market for publically traded REITS are more liquid and offers you quick and easy exit when you need to go to cash.

Frequently Asked Questions and Answers

- What is an REIT?
  - This is a company that mainly owns income-generating real estate and distributes its earnings to shareholders.

- What types of REITs are there?
  - REITs are often placed into two categories: equity REITs and mortgage REITs.

- What kinds of properties do REITs own and operate?
  - These include storage facilities, data centers, timberlands, shopping malls, hotels, office buildings, apartment buildings, warehouses, cell towers, family homes, health care facilities, and shopping centers.

- Can anyone invest in REITs?
  - More or less. Individual investors of all kind are welcome to purchase shares. However, depending on the country, you probably need to be above a certain age to qualify

- What are the benefits of investing in REITs?
  - They provide high dividends plus the potential for capital appreciation.

- How much do REITs pay to shareholders?
  - It depends but you must keep note that REITs are mandated by law to pay 90% of their yearly earnings to shareholders.

- Are returns from REITs taxable?
  - Usually, REITs that distribute 90% of their earnings to shareholders are exempt from paying income taxes. However, we advise you consult your accountant to verify this applies to your specific situation.

- How do I get started investing in REITs?
  - Get in touch with a broker or a financial consultant. They will guide you along the way.

- Why should I have REITs in my portfolio?
  - Because it's a great way to diversify your investments and gain exposure to real estate without doing the less appealing tasks like fixing up houses, toilets etc. It has a very high potential to be passive.

- Are all distributions made by a REIT derived from the REIT's earnings?
  - No. Sometimes, the REIT distributes part of its capital to shareholders.

Myth Busters about Real Estate and REITS

- All tenants are bad. This is not true. If you learn to carefully review rental applications, check references and previous landlords, verify employment and carefully screen tenants you will end up with good tenants most of the time.

- That land is unlimited. On the contrary, land is a limited resource and thus very valuable. Even more so is land in a good location.

- All contractors are thieves. Again, this is not true. The truth is that there are some great reputable contractors who would love to help you rehab some houses. However, they need to be qualified before they can work on your houses. Make sure they are licensed and insured, have great referrals and be sure to document everything with an iron-clad contract.

- That the taxman always wants his cut. You always want to pay your tax but you don't have to overpay. This is why its very important you work closely with your accountant and/or lawyer.

- That it's hard to buy and sell REITs. Knowing when to buy and sell isn't very hard especially when you've educated yourself, you understand the industry and any effect the state of the economy can have on it.

- That owning a REIT is hard work. It need not be. Doing the initial research to decide on which REITS to invest in can be hard work. However, once that initial hard work is done and you're earning it becomes very passive.

- That landlords collect monthly income while REIT investors don't. Not all landlords collect monthly income. Some do on a yearly basis.

- That REITs are restricted to factories, malls, and offices. That's not true. They can also own storage facilities, health care facilities, to name a few.

- The least expensive estate agent is the best value. The agent to select is always the one with the best experience, local market connections, exceptional negotiating skills and a strong pool of buyers. Those don't tend to come cheap.

- That only people with business degrees and extensive real estate experience can invest in REITs. Anyone who is willing to learn and understand how the process works can become a successful real estate investor. A degree is not compulsory

Inspiration #20

"The secret to success is to do the common things uncommonly well."
John D. Rockefeller Jr.

Series #	Book Title
1	Affiliate Marketing
2	Passive Income Ideas
3	Affiliate Marketing + Passive Income Ideas (2-in-1 Bundle)
4	Facebook Advertising
5	Dropshipping
6	Dropshipping + Facebook Advertising (2-in-1 Bundle)
7	Real Estate Investing For Beginners
8	Credit Cards and Credit Repair Secrets
9	Real Estate Investing And Credit Repair Strategies (2-in-1 Bundle)
10	Passive Income Ideas With Affiliate Marketing (2nd Edition)
11	Passive Income With Dividend Investing
12	Stock Market Investing For Beginners
13	The Simple Stock Market Investing Blueprint (2-in-1 Bundle)
14	Real Estate And Stock Market Investing Mastery (3-in-1 Bundle)
15	Amazon FBA Mastery

Business #20

Become a Business Silent Partner

First of all, what is a business silent partner? A silent partner is usually an individual whose involvement in the business is limited to providing capital. He is seldom involved in the management and day-to-day operations of the business. As a partner in the business, the silent partner shares in the income. For example, let's say that a friend of yours is opening a coffee shop. He needs additional capital so he invites you to become a silent partner.

You agree and provide the additional capital with the agreement that you are going to share in the profits. Of course, this is just the tip of the iceberg. The deal between you and your friend can include other factors that may pertain to operations and management. But the bottom line is that your involvement in the business is often limited to providing capital.

Ratings Based on Our Criteria

A. **Simplicity:**
Becoming a silent partner is quite simple especially if you know and trust the business owner.
7/10

B. **Passivity:**
Once you recover the capital you infused in the business, every dollar that goes your way is pretty much passive income, as you're not actively exchanging your time for the money.
8/10

C. **Scalability:**
To scale your earnings, you have to either increase the size/ownership percentage of your current investments or invest in more businesses as a silent partner.
6/10

D. **Competitiveness:**
If your terms are favorable, there's little or no competition unless there are other people trying to become silent partners with the business owner.
6/10

Tips For Success

- Only enter into business partnerships with people you trust.
- Only invest in businesses that you think will be profitable. Don't invest in a business just because you know the owner.
- Make sure that you understand each other's commitments and responsibilities.
- Make sure that all the technical aspects of the deal and contract are documented and put into paper.
- Decide on your percentage share of the profits.
- Decide if you are going to get a fixed or a flexible percentage share in the profits.
- Make a provision in the contract that you have the right to request or look into the financial sheets of the business.
- Stay in touch with the business owner whenever you can.
- Have the contract checked by your lawyer before you sign it.
- Keep a separate record of all the contributions you've invested into the business.

Frequently Asked Questions and Answers

- What is a silent partner?
  - A silent partner is an individual who invests in a business by providing capital but isn't involved in the operation and management of the business.

- How does a silent partner benefit from the business?
  - He gets a percentage share in the profits of the business.

- Can a silent partner have a say in the operation and management of the business?
  - The silent partner is rarely involved in these activities but if it's stipulated in the contract that he can get involved, then he has the right to be involved.

- How much is the percentage share of the silent partner?
  - It depends on what was stipulated in the contract but the share is usually decided upon based on the silent partner's capital contribution.

- Can a silent partner exit from the business?
  - Yes, as long as it's stipulated in the contract that he has exit options.

- Does the silent partner also share in the losses?
  - Yes, he shares losses in the same way that he shares in the profits.

- What are the limitations of being a silent partner?
  - You have very little involvement in the operation and management of the business.

- Can a silent partner invest more capital in the business after his initial investment?
  - Yes, if it's stipulated in the contract that he can do so.

- Will the silent partner receive a salary on top of his shares in the profits?
  - It's very rare for silent partners to receive salaries. They usually only share in the profits.

- Can I be a silent partner in numerous businesses?
  - Yes, there's no law prohibiting you from investing in as many businesses as you can.

Myth Busters about Silent Partners in Business

- That you need a lot of money to invest in a business as a silent partner. How much you need to invest will depend on the value of the business.

- That you can't invest as silent partner in several businesses. Such restrictions usually don't exist unless there's a stipulation in a previous partnership contract that demands exclusivity.

- That being a silent partner is a waste of one's time. On the contrary, partnering with someone can save you a lot of time if you have the money to invest but not the time to get bogged down with the day-to-day operation of a business.

- That you will lose a lot of money investing as a silent partner. It can go both ways. You can win big as well as lose big. Carefully analyzing the proposal and the business owner's management skills will help reduce the risk of failure and maximize the proportion of your investments that turn out to be profitable.

- That it's always better to start your own business than invest as a silent partner. This depends on your situation. Like I said earlier, if you have the money to invest but not the time to be hands-on with the business, then this option will most likely suit you.

- That silent partners have zero say in the operation and management of the business. How much say you have in the management of the business will depend on what's stipulated in the contract between you and the business owner.

- That silent partners can be easily kicked out of the partnership by the main owner of the business. Again, this depends on the terms of agreement as stipulated in the contract. Make sure to have your lawyer look through the fine print to make sure there're no surprises.

- That you can't increase your shares in the profits if you're a silent partner. What you can and cannot do will depend on what's stipulated in the contract you signed with the business owner.

- That you can't renegotiate the stipulations in the original contract. You can if it says so in the contract.

- That you can't make good money as a silent partner. Your ability to make money will depend on your ability to spot good investment opportunities and your judgment when it comes to partnering with the right people.

Inspiration #21
"I failed my way to success."
Thomas Edison

Business #21

Rent Out Unused Space with AirBnb

If there's unused space in your home or apartment, you can earn extra passive income from it by listing the space on Airbnb. Signing up with Airbnb will take just a few minutes of your time. You have full control on how much you rent out your unused space.

Airbnb offers their services in 191 countries and nearly 90,000 cities. Chances are it's available in your location. However, you should keep in mind that Airbnb gets a cut from the transactions you process through their online marketplace. The company charges a 3% fee that covers the cost of processing the transactions.

Ratings Based on Our Criteria

A. **Simplicity:**
It's quite simple. List your unused space on Airbnb and wait for anyone to rent it.
9/10

B. **Passivity:**
Most of the income you earn from your unused space are passive income.
8/10

C. **Scalability:**
To scale your earnings, you need to find more spaces and properties to rent out.
5/10

D. **Competitiveness:**
It can be very competitive if you live in an urban area that's teeming with tourists and outsiders.
3/10

Tips For Success

- Prepare the space and make it as comfortable as possible.
- Provide as many amenities as possible.
- Take high-quality photos when creating your listing on Airbnb.
- Encourage your guests to leave reviews and comments.
- Offer an individualized experience. Talk and interact with your guests.
- Offer a reasonable price. Don't underprice or overprice your space.
- Be quick in responding to questions and comments.
- Make your listing as descriptive and detailed as possible.
- Be very honest when making your listings. Don't say there's Wi-Fi if there's not.
- Assure your guests of security. You may be able to command a higher rent if your guests know that when they stay in your space, they'll be safe and that their belongings won't be stolen or anything.

Frequently Asked Questions and Answers

- How much does Airbnb take from you?
    - Airbnb takes a 3% fee from your transactions.

- How does payment work on Airbnb?

  - Depends on the payment method. You can either get paid via credit cards, PayPal, Alipay, Postepay, etc.

- How much money can I earn from Airbnb?
  - If you make $4000 a month from an apartment, your take-home pay is usually half after taking into account the Airbnb fees, utilities and other expenses.

- How much does it cost to list a space for rent on Airbnb?
  - Creating a listing is free. You only get charged a fee when someone books your space.

- Is it necessary to ask for a deposit from guests?
  - Most hosts require a security deposit but it's not mandatory.

- How do I deal with guests who cancel their reservations?
  - You should create a cancellation policy for your listed spaces.

- Can I list multiple spaces with different hosting policies?
  - Yes you can as long as you are following Airbnb's own listing policies and regulations.

- What's a cleaning fee?
  - This is a fee that the host collects to help cover incidents incurred during a stay such as broken items, damaged furniture, or unreturned keys.

- Can you be an Airbnb host even if you are a renter yourself?
  - It's possible but you have to talk to your landlord first to make sure that they are okay with it.

- What are the responsibilities of an Airbnb host?
  - Deliver the services that you promised in the listing you made on Airbnb.

Myth Busters about Renting Out Space in Airbnb

- That if you list it, guests will start coming. That's not always the case, you still need to optimize your listings with use quality pictures, earn good reviews, offer competitive rates and promote your listings.

- That it's very expensive to list a space in Airbnb. Listing is free. You're only charged when your space is booked.

- That you can earn more from your space if you advertise it yourself and not list it on Airbnb. Taking charge of the advertising or hiring an agent to help you find a client will probably cost you more as opposed to leveraging the Airbnb platform, their global reputation and established database of clients looking to rent etc. all for a small service fee.

- That it's not secure to transact with strangers on Airbnb. Payments are made on Airbnb via a secure payment system.

- That the cost of running an Airbnb space is more than the earnings you make from your efforts. That's not the case. Airbnb charges hosts a 3% fee that covers the cost of processing payments

- That Airbnb has hidden fees you don't know about. In most cases, guests are made aware of all fees, including service charges and taxes, prior to confirming their decision to book a listing.

- That Airbnb is selling your personal information to other companies. Airbnb may collect your personal information in order to help improve customer service, personalize user experience, to process payment etc. However, its highly unlikely they'll sell that information to other companies without your express permission. That would be against the law.

- That you can't create multiple listings on Airbnb. If you want to list multiple rooms in your house, you can create a separate listing for each space you have available. Each room will have its own calendar and listing page that should accurately reflect the number of beds and amenities available.

- That it's illegal to rent out your apartment if you are renting it yourself. The legality of this will depend on the agreement you have with the owner of the house.

- That the Airbnb service fee is non-refundable. According to information on the Airbnb website, the service fee is refundable up to 3 times per year if you cancel within 48 hours of booking the reservation (as of July 2018)

Inspiration #22

"The only place where success comes before work is in the dictionary."

Vidal Sassoon

Business #22

Invest in a Lending Club

The business model for Lending Club is quite straightforward. There are borrowers who are looking for unsecured loans through the site. As an investor and a lender, you can browse through these loan listings and find those that you would like to lend to. Needless to say, you make money from interest returns.

Investing in Lending Club is a great way to earn passive income if you have cash that you can lend. Interest rates range from 6% to 26% depending on the credit grades assigned to the borrowers requesting for a personal loan. What's great about Lending Club's business model is that you have the freedom to choose the loans you want to invest in.

Ratings Based on Our Criteria

A. **Simplicity:**
Investing in loan listings in a Lending Club is simple. Just sign up as an investor and start browsing through the loan requests.

8/10

B. **Passivity:**
Almost 100% of the interest you earn are passive income.

9/10

C. **Scalability:**
To scale, you simply have to invest in more loan requests.

8/10

D. **Competitiveness:**
There are thousands of other investors in Lending Club so competition can be tough which can potentially drive down interest rates.

4/10

Tips For Success

- Since loans are unsecured, defaults are bound to happen so you may want to diversify your account across multiple notes.

- Keep your account fully invested. As your loans get repaid, your cash reserve will begin to build up. This idle cash earns no interest so you have to keep reinvesting or your overall return will decrease. The easiest way to stay fully invested is to activate Lending Club's Automated Investing tool.

- Strategically increase the risk in your portfolio. The more risk you take the more return you earn on your invested dollar. However, you will need to choose the level of risk that is appropriate for your risk tolerance. In a bad economy, the unemployment rate goes up, so more borrowers than normal default on their loans. If you're good at tracking the state of the economy, it might be a good idea to take more risk when the economy is doing well and reduce your exposure when key performance indicators (from Bloomberg, Reuters etc.) show that the economy might be struggling.

- Filter for loans with no previous inquiries.

- Invest through an IRA. Taxes can have a detrimental effect on peer-to-peer investments. Investing through an IRA (which is essentially a tax free account), will allow you to save more money.

- Don't be greedy and expose yourself to too much unnecessary risk.

- Always endeavor to learn from your previous investments (good or bad) in order to understand what strategy is working for you and do more of it or learn from mistakes and avoid them in the future.

- Take the time to research about a borrower before you grant him/her a loan.

- Take the borrowers job security into account. When selecting notes to invest in, don't just look at how much money someone makes. Take a look at what the person does for a living and how long they've been doing it. Government employees with a decade of experience are much less likely to experience a bout of unemployment.

- Pay attention to the reasons for borrowing, as this can often be predictive of default rates. Is the borrower looking to get a loan to cover vacation, weddings, medical costs or home improvements? On average, loans to cover home improvements have an average default rate of 3.5% while those for educational expenses have an average default rate of 5%.

Frequently Asked Questions and Answers

- How does Lending Club work?
  - Borrowers create loan listings and requests on the site. As an investor, you get to choose which of these loan applications you want to invest in.

- How do you make money from Lending Club?
  - You earn money through interest in your investments.

- How do I choose which notes to buy?
  - Consider information like loan grade, purpose, term, debt to income ratio, and credit score.

- How do I get returns on my capital and interest?
  - Whenever monthly payments by borrowers are received and then disbursed by the company.

- Can I reinvest or withdraw my capital and interest earnings?
  - Yes, any time you want to.

- How do I withdraw my money?
  - You can withdraw available cash to your bank account any time you like.

- What if a borrower misses a payment?
  - Lending Club deal with delinquencies. You don't have to do anything.

- How do I improve returns on my investments?
  - Follow an investing plan to increase your returns while minimizing the risks.

- Are my earnings taxable?
  - Yes, they are taxable as regular income.

- Are my investments insured?
  - Your account cash balance is covered by FDIC insurance up to the limits put forth by the FDIC.

Myth Busters about Investing in Lending Club

- That because the loans are unsecured, there's more risks than returns. You can significantly reduce your risks by diversifying and analyzing notes closely before investing.

- That investing is only for millionaires. On the contrary, being a millionaire isn't necessary. You can invest as little as $25. All that's required is that you know what you're doing. Seek to educate yourself, work with mentors who are successful peer-to-peer investors, learn from their mistakes and your mistakes.

- That it's safer to invest $1000 than invest $10,000. Regardless of how much you invest you can lose it all if you invest carelessly (without any education, due diligence etc.)

- That it's illegal or it's within the confines of a grey market. Peer-to-peer lending platforms are not illegal

- That the company doesn't have a clear business model. The company has a clear business model which you can find on their website

- That the company doesn't care about its lenders. The company has been around since 2007. It definitely wouldn't survive that long if it didn't care about its lenders. Part of their commitment is to deliver world class experience to borrowers and investors alike

- That the returns are too low compared to the risks involved. The more risk you take the more return you can potentially get on your money. Invest strategically (i.e. doing your due diligence, screening notes carefully prior to investing, diversifying your portfolio etc.) and you can potentially get the good returns while not risking too much.

- That you are always better off investing your money somewhere else. That's not always the case. Sometimes, you can find better ROI opportunities on peer-to-peer platforms than other places.

- That online loan applications are confusing and too complicated. Lending Club has made significant progress with regards to simplifying this process.

- That borrowers need high credit scores to be approved. Credit scores are not the only criteria when it comes to making lending decisions. Other factors like job security can play a major role.

Inspiration #23

"Keep on going, and the chances are that you will stumble on something, perhaps when you are least expecting it. I never heard of anyone ever stumbling on something sitting down."

Charles F. Kettering

Business #23

Get Cash Back Rewards on Credit Cards

Using a cashback rewards credit card is a nice way to get back a percentage of your purchases. If you do a lot of your shopping online or if you use your credit card often, you should consider making use of one that offers cashback rewards. A cashback is basically a rebate of a percentage of the purchases you make on the card. There are three main types of cashback reward cards. These are category bonus cashback cards, tiered rewards cashback cards, and simple cashback cards.

Ratings Based on Our Criteria

A. **Simplicity:**
Simply use your cashback reward credit card when you do your shopping.
8/10

B. **Passivity:**
The rebates you receive from your credit cards can be considered as passive income.
8/10

C. **Scalability:**
To get more rebates, you need to use your cards more often.
5/10

D. **Competitiveness:**
There's little or no competition here.
9/10

Tips For Success

- Align rewards with your interests and goals. For example, if travelling is your thing, you should get a rewards card for airline miles.

- Make sure that the products and services you are purchasing are covered by your rewards card. Keep in mind that there are always exemptions.

- Pay attention to the annual fees because cards with the highest rewards often collect the highest annual fees.

- Skip cards with excess restrictions. An excess restriction means you can no longer earn rewards when you reach a certain amount of purchases.

- Look for sign-up bonuses. A sign-up bonus can be akin to free money.

- Use multiple cards if possible. More rewards cards means you have access to more products and services that have cashbacks.

- Take advantage of bonus offers if these are offered by your credit card provider.

- Make your purchases through online shopping malls because these often have partnerships with credit card providers.

- Make the most of bill pay options. Use your credit card to pay for your bills if you get rebates on your payments.

- Keep your spending in check. Getting more rebates doesn't always mean you are saving or earning money.

Frequently Asked Questions and Answers

- What is a cashback rewards credit card?
  - This is a credit card that offers rebates on your purchases.

- Which credit cards have the highest cashback rewards?
  - These would be Discover, Wells Fargo Cash Wise, Citi Double Cash, Chase Freedom, and Capital One Quicksilver One.

- How does a cashback work?
  - Every time you use the card, you earn a percentage of your purchase in the form of a cashback.

- Can I keep several cashback cards at the same time?
  - Yes, you can.

- What stores can I get a cashback?
  - These would include Staples, Rite-Aid, Walgreens, Whole Foods, and Best Buy.

- Is there such a thing as a 100% cashback?
  - Yes, sometimes credit card companies would offer 100% cashback for certain items and transactions.

- When do I receive a cashback?
  - Usually during the point of sale or when your points accumulate over time until you get to claim your rewards.

- Do cashback credit cards come with annual fees?
  - Yes, most of them collect annual dues.

- Are there any excess restrictions?
  - Some cards stop offering cashbacks when you reach their maximum limitation.

- How about minimum purchases?
  - Some credit cards also apply their rewards system only when you reach the minimum amount of purchases.

Myth Busters about Using Cashback Credit Cards

- That credit card rewards are easy to redeem. They can be if you make an effort to always pay attention to the fine print. You need to make sure you fully understand the conditions under which the rewards apply.

- That pursuing rewards will ruin your credit score. It need not be. When done correctly, the impact on your credit score is minimal.

- That you are actually paying for those miles. You partially pay for some of the miles since you have to spend to qualify. However, you don't pay for the complete mile.

- That credit card rewards make travel free. This is true only when used properly. Some people are so good at the credit card game they're able to finance around-the-globe travels almost entirely on points alone.

- That credit card rewards are not worth the effort. How useful the rewards are to you will depend on your lifestyle. Using cash or debit cards to pay when you could be earning reward points with a credit card means throwing money away – money that adds up over the long haul.

- That applying for a reward credit card will hurt your credit score. It's true that inquiries stemming from a credit card application can have a negative effect on your credit scores, but in most cases the effect is minimal, and any effect they do have is temporary.

- That cancelling your credit cards will improve your credit score. Having a good credit score depends on many factors, one of which is the age of your credit history. Cancelling old credit cards can reduce the age of your credit history – negatively impacting your credit score.

- That earning points and miles is a waste of time. It depends on the person's situation. This type of reward is especially useful for those people who travel a lot.

- That you can't just apply for a credit card to get the sign-up bonus. You can do this. However, bare in mind this can significantly affect your credit score. Everything you do with credit cards, from applying to closing them, impacts your credit rating. A hard inquiry will be placed on your reports soon after you applied, which would shave a few points from your score.

- That you can carry a balance and still earn rewards. More often than not, these rewards are conditional on you not carrying a balance. Moreover, paying interest on a credit balance can negate the effect of the reward.

Inspiration #24

"Your time is limited, so don't waste it living someone else's life."

Steve Jobs

Business #24

Create a Comparison Website

If you regularly purchase products online, I'm sure that you've come across a comparison website. A comparison website is sometimes called a comparison shopping engine, shopbot, comparison shopping agent, or price analysis tool. The main function of a comparison website is to offer online shoppers the ability to compare products based on price, reviews, features, and other criteria. What a comparison website usually does is collect and aggregate data from various online shopping sites then present the information in the form of a comparison table.

How does a comparison website make money? Most comparison websites earn through affiliate marketing. If an online shopper clicks on a product link on the comparison website, he gets redirected to Amazon or eBay or any online shopping portal. If the shopper ends up buying the product, the comparison website earns an affiliate commission. As you can see, this business model can be lucrative if your comparison website gets a lot of traffic.

You can create the comparison website yourself. Or you can hire a web developer to do it for you if you don't have the necessary coding and programming skills. Affiliate marketing isn't the only way to make money from a comparison website. You can also earn through advertising and sponsored listings. This free webinar by the legendary online marketer, Kevin David, shows you the power of using Facebook Ads to identify the ideal customers for your business and drive them to your website at a fraction of the cost.

Ratings Based on Our Criteria

A. **Simplicity:**
Creating and maintaining a comparison website can be hard especially if you are not that technically savvy.

5/10

B. **Passivity:**
Majority of the income you earn from a comparison website is passive income. However, it may require a lot of time commitment since you need to regularly update your comparisons of products – unless you use software to automate this.

7/10

C. **Scalability:**
To scale your earnings, you need to double the number of entries in your website or you create another one.

7/10

D. **Competitiveness:**
There are a lot of general comparison websites so competition can be tough. However, you can avoid much of this by going into a specific niche.

4/10

Tips For Success

- Do your research first before you jump into the fray.
- You can hire a professional web developer from upwork.com or fiverr.com if you are not a developer yourself.
- Consider focusing on a specific niche. Most of the competition are general comparison websites.

- Sign up with as many affiliate programs as you can.
- Hire freelance writers to regularly create content for your comparison website.
- Make your website mobile-friendly.
- Promote your website on major social media platforms.
- Run contests and promos on social media platforms to attract visitors.
- Optimize your website for search engines.
- Set aside a budget for advertising campaigns.

Frequently Asked Questions and Answers

- What is a comparison website?
  - This is a website that collects and compares products from various online shopping stores.

- How do comparison websites earn money?
  - Mostly through affiliate marketing.

- What is affiliate marketing?
  - This is an online marketing model which involves promoting products by other companies and earning commissions from your sales and referrals.

- Is it difficult to operate and maintain a comparison website?
  - Yes, it can take a lot of your time because you need to regularly update your comparisons of products.

- How much does it cost to build a comparison website?
  - It depends on factors like the size of the website and if you are hiring a team of developers.

- Where can I find products to compare in my website?
  - Make use of popular online shopping portals like Amazon, eBay, Walmart, Target, etc.

- Do I need software to run a comparison website?
  - Yes, you do. You can have the software created by a freelancer or you can purchase software being sold in the market.

- How much money can I earn from a comparison website?
  - It depends on the size, scope, and popularity of your website. Some comparison websites earn up to six figures a month.

- Aside from affiliate marketing, are there other ways to monetize a comparison website?
  - Yes, you can use advertising and sponsorships.

- How do I promote my comparison website?
  - Get active with social media marketing, search engine optimization, and advertising.

Myth Busters about Building a Comparison Website

- That it's easy to build a comparison website. If you're tech savvy yes. If not, it can be a challenge unless you happen to know a good web developer – but this will cost you.

- That building a comparison website is not worth it because of the competition. Most business opportunities have competition. You should go in with the mindset to be better than the competition.

- That you can't create a comparison website if you're not a developer or coder. You can always outsource this to someone who can develop the site for you.

- That it's very expensive to create a comparison website. How expensive it is will depend on may factors like the complexity of the site, whether you're using a site builder like wix, godaddy, weebly or hiring a web developer, cost of maintenance etc.

- That it's very difficult to monetize a comparison website. Like I mentioned earlier, you can easily monetize your comparison site with sponsored listings and affiliate products.

- That affiliate marketing is the only way to monetize a comparison website. You can also use sponsored listings, selling advertising space for banner, display and text ads, inviting third-party suppliers to pay a subscription fee in order to feature on your site etc.

- That a comparison website is useless because consumers can just compare the products themselves. This can be very time consuming. Comparison sites, by their very nature, are there to make things easier.

- That you don't need software and apps for a comparison website. You need software to automate some of the processes. Failure to do this erodes the passivity of this business model.

- That comparison websites don't offer updated and accurate information about products. Sometimes, sites that are updated manually may be guilty of this. However, comparison sites that have been set up to update automatically provide more accurate and reliable information.

- That comparison websites are manipulating price lists to make money off their visitors. This would be illegal. While we cannot speak for every price comparison site out there, the majority of them make money via the avenues we discussed earlier e.g. affiliate marketing, sponsored listing etc.

Inspiration #25

"Paying attention to simple little things that most men neglect makes a few men rich."

Henry Ford

Secret Bonus Offer

Congratulations on getting this far! You are a very motivated person and, seeing as not a lot of people actually bother to read a book once they purchase it (much less read more than 200 pages), you are definitely one in a million! Here's my small reward to you. Go to https://michaelezeanaka.com/download/getting-started-online/ to download my Getting Started Online guide. The password for the download is **passive** (all lower case letters)

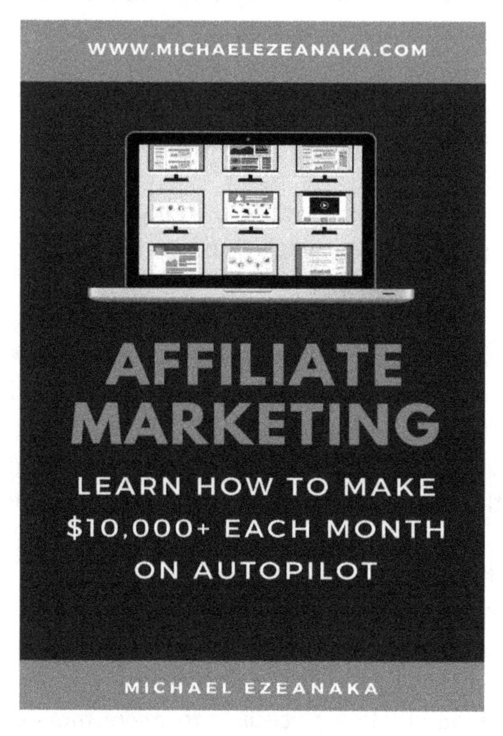

In addition, when you purchase the paperback version of this book, you'll receive (at the very end of the paperback) the password and instructions required to download the PDF version of my bestselling book – Affiliate Marketing: Learn How to Make $10,000+ Each Month on Autopilot. Not many people know about this so let's keep this a secret between us ☺

Finally, please kindly leave a review for this book letting me know what you loved about it and which business model in particular resonated with you the most.

Business #25

Create a Software Program

If you have skills in programming and coding, you can create your own software program which you then sell to interested buyers. There are numerous ways on how you can monetize your skill as a software programmer. You can offer your services as a freelancer. You can create the program then sell it per download or offer it with a subscription business model. There's a huge market for practical software programs out there. Your clients can be individual entrepreneurs, companies, government agencies, non-profit organizations, educational institutions, gaming companies, and even medical institutions.

The trick to finding a good idea for a profitable software is to look for practical problems out there that are in need of a solution. For example, let's say that you have a hard time organizing the PDF files in your computer. What if you can create a piece of software that allows you to separate them into several categories with just a click of a button? What if you can create a software that enables you to easily access a PDF file by merely entering a keyword into a search bar? In a nutshell, find simple problems that a lot of people have, and try to solve it with a software.

Ratings Based on Our Criteria

A. **Simplicity:**
I wouldn't call software programming simple. It's a time-consuming endeavor.
4/10

B. **Passivity:**
Once your software is finished and launched, most of the income you earn from it is passive.
7/10

C. **Scalability:**
To scale the business, you have to create more programs or make your existing programs available on a lot more platforms and to more people.
7/10

D. **Competitiveness:**
The software industry is very competitive. You are up against both freelance programmers and programmers working for million-dollar companies.
3/10

Tips For Success

- Work on projects that you are passionate about and have proven demand
- The software industry evolves at a very fast pace. To stay ahead, you need to continue learning and upgrading your skill set.
- Connect, network and learn from other programmers.
- Try to learn as many programming relevant languages as you can. This will help you diversify your options incase one programming language is no longer in high demand
- Write clean code that you can reuse over and over again and other people will understand.
- Focus on projects that have commercial value for businesses.
- Focus on functionality and practicality.
- Collaborate with other programmers.

- Do not market yourself with just one specialization.
- Understand and be updated about current technology trends.

Frequently Asked Questions and Answers

- What does a software developer do?
  - Their responsibilities include reviewing current systems, maintaining systems, testing software, improving software, and creating software specifications.

- Who hires software developers?
  - As a software developer, you can work independently as a freelancer or you can work for design and technology firms.

- Which types of coding languages should you know?
  - The most common programming languages include C++, Java, Visual Basic, PHP/MySQL, HTML, CSS, and Ruby on Rails.

- How to increase your chances of getting hired?
  - Get as much experience as you can to improve your portfolio.

- Where can I find jobs for software developers?
  - There are numerous online job sites that you can use such as Freelancer, Odesk, Fiverr, Upwork and Craigslist.

- How much does a freelance software developer earns?
  - It depends. A large number of freelancers earn up to six figures a year.

- How competitive is the demand for software developers?
  - It can be tough so you need to get a lot of experience so you can show a better portfolio and resume.

- How do I market myself as a software developer?
  - Follow basic online marketing strategies like search engine optimization, social media marketing, content marketing, advertising, etc.

- Do I need to create an online portfolio?
  - Yes, you have to.

- Should I have my own website?
  - Yes, a website is a great place for you to talk about your skills and experiences as a software developer.

Myth Busters about Software Development

- That software development comes with a hefty price tag. You can develop software for a relatively low price. How much you spend will depend on the complexity of the software and/or who you hire to develop it.

- That software development has a fixed cost and a strict timeframe. There's rarely a fixed cost when it comes to software development. Unexpected things happen and adjustments need to be made. However, since this is rare, your ability to consistently stay on budget and meet a set timeframe will enable you to command a premium price as a developer or software company.

- That when the software is released, the project is over. You need to take on customer feedback, continually test the software to fix bugs and release updates.
- That outsourcing solves everything. It doesn't. You still need to make sure you outsource to capable people
- That outsourcing means compromising quality. There are very talented software developers out there looking for work. The key to developing quality software using freelancers is finding these people.
- That software development is a predictable process. It is anything but predictable. Problems do occur during the development stage and good entrepreneurs adapt accordingly.
- That adding more people to the project will speed things up. Quantity doesn't necessarily equate to quality. If you're going to hire more people, you need to make sure they're capable and everyone in the team is well informed with regards to what other people in the team are doing. Effective collaboration is key.
- That software development is all about coding. It's not. At the end of the day, if you're unable to market the software you develop, you can't sell it.
- That there is a silver bullet software development methodology. There isn't
- That adding extra features at any point of the project isn't a big deal. Adding extra features require thorough regression and positive testing to ensure they work as intended. This can have a tremendous effect on the team's ability to meet its deadlines. It's probably better to add features at the beginning of the development when there's still a lot of time to adjust to setbacks than to add features closer to the deadline.

Inspiration #26

"Formal education will make you a living; self education will make you a fortune."

Jim Rohn

Business #26

Buy and Rent Out Expensive Equipment

Many people are often in need of expensive equipment that they are only going to use once or twice e.g. construction equipment, luxury cars for wedding etc. So buying the equipment is often out of the question. They would rather rent than purchase. This is where you enter the picture by creating an equipment rental business. The business model is simple. You purchase expensive equipment and put them up for rent. You can do this both offline and online.

The biggest drawback of starting an equipment rental business is that you are going to need a large capital. A single piece of equipment can cost you a few thousand dollars. Imagine if you get a dozen or so of them. And of course, with a large capital, it's going to take you some time to recover the costs of purchasing the equipment. That said, if you want to be in the equipment rental business, make sure that you are in it for the long haul.

Ratings Based on Our Criteria

A. **Simplicity:**
   The business model is simple but running the business can be hard and time-consuming. Besides the formalities of starting any business, a rental business has extra insurance liabilities. Your entire business depends on non-employees interacting with your equipment.

   6/10

B. **Passivity:**
   For the first months or years, you will be earning back the costs of the equipment. Once that is completed, your earnings become passive income.

   7/10

C. **Scalability:**
   To scale the business, you need to purchase more equipment to rent out.

   6/10

D. **Competitiveness:**
   This is fairly location dependent. Situate your business in a place that has little or no equipment rental businesses to compete with and you'll do well. Otherwise, it'll be a struggle. Furthermore, you can minimize competition by niching down i.e. focusing on specific or unpopular equipments that still have proven demand.

   5/10

Tips For Success

- Study your market. Before you get started, make sure you know what your customers are looking for. What kind of equipment are they looking for – budget or high-end? How much are they willing to pay? Do they need more than rentals i.e. any add-on services?
- Don't buy more, buy smarter. Avoid idle inventory at all cost – it only takes up space and money that you could use to grow your business.
- Find the best deal for your equipment. Can you buy used equipments?
- Get your paperwork in order. Make sure you have the right insurance.
- Stake your claim online. It's vital that you have an online presence.

- Create partnerships. What other products or services are your customers looking for? Contact the companies that offer these services and ask them if they would be interested in a referral partnership
- Find the right tools for your business. Accounting software, communication tool kit etc.
- Treat your equipment right. Spot and fix potential problems before your customers do.
- Treat your customers well. Create a hassle-free experience
- Create a waterproof agreement. Make sure you and your customers are on the same page

Frequently Asked Questions and Answers

- How do I get started in the equipment rental business?
  - First of all you need to decide on which kind of equipment you are going to rent out. Get your business plan in place and register it with the proper government agency.

- How much capital do I need?
  - It depends on the equipment you are going to rent out. Capital can be as low as $30,000 and can be as high as $1 million.

- How do I collect payments?
  - Payments are usually done in cash, credit card, or check.

- How much should I charge for the equipment?
  - It depends on the equipment and for how long the customer is going to use it.

- What if a customer doesn't return an equipment?
  - You should set up policies, regulations, and penalties about overdue and unreturned equipment.

- How do I promote the business?
  - If it's a local business, try putting out advertisements in the local paper or radio. You can also try promoting your business online especially on social media.

- How about taxes?
  - Since you are a registered business, you need to pay your taxes.

- Do I need a partner in the business?
  - Starting an equipment rental business can be costly. You should consider getting partners to help in providing the needed capital.

- How about insurance?
  - It's important that you insure all of your business equipment as a buffer against disasters.

- How do I deal with equipment damaged by clients?
  - You need to come up with rules, regulations, and penalties that cover damaged equipment.

Myth Busters about Renting Out Equipment

- That it's easy to start an equipment rental business. That will depend on your level of expertise going into this business. If you're a complete novice, you'll need to, among other things, conduct adequate research and proper niche selection.

- That you don't have to buy insurance for your equipment. You absolutely need to if you want to protect yourself from potentially catastrophic losses.

- That you can only cater to a local clientele. This depends on the nature of the equipment you're renting. While something light and portable could lend itself to a larger market, something big and heavy may not.

- That it will take years before you start earning profits from the rentals. Your breakeven point will depend on a lot of factors such as how much you invested in purchasing the equipment, how much rent you charge for it, how much you're paying in insurance premium and equipment maintenance etc. Get the balance right and you may breakeven a lot quicker.

- That it's a waste of time to try and promote the business online. Chances are a lot of your clients will have social media accounts and will spend some time there. Being able to put your offer in front of them will give you an edge over your competitors.

- That a rental business is not worth the huge capital you need to get started. This depends on how well you've researched the market before going in. Is there demand for the equipment you're looking to purchase? Have you conducted a survey to determine what your ideal customers are willing to pay in rent? Will this rent amount be enough to make you profitable in the long haul? Like any business, if you fail to prepare, you prepare to fail.

- That the equipment will break down before they even recur their costs. This can be avoided with proper and regular maintenance

- That you can only rent over a long-term basis. On the contrary, rental terms are very flexible. You can arrange for the terms that suit your situation.

- That the risks are too high. The inherent risk can be managed if you have the right knowledge. You need to understand what your customers want, the equipment that are in demand, where to locate your business and how to properly insure your equipment.

- That the equipment rental market is saturated and thus too competitive. With the right location, good customer research and proper niche selection, you can avoid unnecessary competition.

Inspiration #27

"Stopping advertising to save money is like stopping your watch to save time."

Henry Ford

Business #27

Buy an Existing Online Business

Why start a business from scratch when you can just buy one that's already been established? This is the concept behind the idea of scouring the internet for businesses that are up for sale. These are usually online businesses whose owners simply don't have the time in operating and managing them. These can be in the form of authority websites, forums, affiliate sites, membership websites, subscription-based websites, Amazon FBA businesses, and so on and so forth. To find these businesses for sale, you need to search for listings in online marketplaces like Flippa.

Ratings Based on Our Criteria

A. **Simplicity:**
It's definitely much simpler than starting a business from scratch. Online marketplaces like Flippa.com have made it relatively easy to filter out the businesses that match your interest and make a fairly informed purchase decision based on their key performance indicators.
8/10

B. **Passivity:**
Passivity of your earnings will depend on the nature of the business you purchase.
6/10

C. **Scalability:**
To scale the business, you need to buy more businesses or expand your operations.
6/10

D. **Competitiveness:**
The competition for established businesses that are for sale can be tough. You can have a lot of people bidding to have their hands on the same business you're interested in.
4/10

Tips For Success

- Only buy a business with a good track record.
- Try to request for a copy of the previous financial statements of the business.
- Is it an evergreen business? To be an evergreen business, it has to be profitable all year round as opposed to something seasonal.
- Check out the products and services of the business if they're updated and still saleable.
- Ask if the business has ever been flagged for illegal or unethical practices. What's the owner's reason for selling?
- Check and read reviews by former customers of the business.
- Check all the legal documents associated with the business before you sign the deal.
- Make sure that the business doesn't have any outstanding debts or payables before you take it over.
- Only buy businesses in niches and industries that you are familiar with. Or at least consult first with someone knowledgeable about the business.
- Make improving and growing the business your main objectives.

Myths About Buying An Existing Business

- That you could never afford it. You'll be surprised that many businesses could be affordable if you're willing to downsize, reel in incredulous spending, and make smart personal and business decisions.

- That it's too much of a risk. You can minimize the risk by doing your due diligence, hiring the services of professionals (accountants, lawyers etc.) to look over the financials presented by the seller and the agreement fine print to make sure all is in order.

- That it's too much work. You aren't the first person to purchase a pre-existing business or franchise – many tools for streamlining the process exist.

- That you don't need to worry about the seller after the sale. Thought must be given to whether a buyer expects a seller to refrain from working in the industry, and to be sure the seller agrees to these terms. Don't just rely on the seller's assurance that they'll retire after the sale. Get that in writing if it's important that they don't end up being your competitor after the sale

Inspiration #28

"We are what we repeatedly do. Excellence then is not an act but a habit."

Aristotle

Business #28

License Out Your Smart Ideas and Earn Royalties

Let's say you have a great idea for a gadget which you think has the potential of finding a market. You did your research, you determined that it's an original idea, and you're determined to make money out of it. However, you don't have the money nor the resources to create the gadget and bring it to market yourself. This is where you should consider licensing your idea. In licensing your idea, you are basically renting out your intellectual property.

When you license your idea, there's another player in the transaction called the "licensee". The licensee is the company who has the ability to manufacture your product and bring it to market. They have the money, the tools, the manpower, and the resources that you don't have. They manufacture and distribute your product with the intention of generating profits for all parties involved. The licensee puts a markup on the cost of manufacturing and distributing the product. This is how they earn from the deal. You on the other hand earn royalties from sales of the product.

How do royalty payments work? Your royalty payment is a percentage of the product's wholesale cost. Let's say that the licensee spent $1 to manufacture the product then sold it to the retailer for $3. The retailer then sold the product to a customer for $6. Your royalty will be based on the wholesale cost of $3. If your royalty percentage is 5%, then you earn a royalty of 15 cents for every product sold.

Ratings Based on Our Criteria

A. **Simplicity:**
The business model is easy to understand and follow. As long as you can find a licensee to rent out your ideas, you're good to go.

8/10

B. **Passivity:**
Royalties are purely passive income.

10/10

C. **Scalability:**
To scale, you must come up with more ideas that you license out.

6/10

D. **Competitiveness:**
If your idea is original and/or legally protected, you may face little or no competition. However, bare in mind you might compete with other substitute ideas that are similar but not exactly the same as yours.

5/10

Tips For Success

- Do extensive research about your idea to make sure that it's truly original. Problems can arise down the road if other people start claiming that the idea is theirs.

- Find a licensee that fits your product category. If you have an idea for a kitchen gadget, don't bring it to a licensee that specializes in car parts.

- You should consider working with a licensing agent. A licensing agent is a professional who specializes in connecting idea originators with a proper licensee.

- Polish your sales pitch before you contact a potential licensee. Make sure that your proposal is flawless before you pick up the phone to set up an appointment.

- Call the licensee first and talk to someone who deals with sales pitches and product proposals. Don't just barge into the company's headquarters.

- Come up with a presentation that completely covers all aspects of your product idea. Present sketches of the product, descriptions of the features, the materials they will be made of, etc.

- Try making a rough prototype of your idea. Studies show that idea proposals with prototypes have higher approvals compared to proposals without a prototype.

- Follow up with the company after making your pitch. Gather the courage to call them and inquire if they are still interested. Being persistent helps.

- Create a backup plan. What if the licensee you visit isn't interested in your idea? You should have a list of other potential licensees that you can approach.

- Negotiate for a higher royalty percentage. If you are confident about the marketability of your idea and you have proof of it e.g. pre-orders, idea goes viral on social media etc., you should request for a higher royalty rate. Sometimes, you just have to ask then fight for it.

Myths About Licensing Your Ideas

- That licensing is complicated. Although some licensing agreements are complex, the process itself is not complicated. At its most basic level, it requires you to prove your intellectual property works, and then finding a partner to license it.

- Licensing is a legal process. That's only a small but important part of it. The essence of licensing is really a marketing and sales process. The more you know about marketing, the better your chance of succeeding.

- Licensing partners are hard to find. Finding the right partner takes time but its not necessarily hard – especially if you know where to look.

Inspiration #29

"What the mind of man can conceive and believe, it can achieve."

Napoleon Hill

Business #29

Invent Something, Have It Patented, and Earn Royalties

In order to profit from your invention, you have to go through the process of patenting it. Whether it's a product, a method, or a device, you need to patent it as soon as possible. Once your patent application has been approved, you will have exclusive property rights over the invention. This prevents competitors from making and selling the product. Patents normally last for twenty (20) years starting from the date you applied for the patent.

After getting the patent, you now have two choices on how to profit from it. You can either sell it or you can license it so that you get to earn recurring royalties. I highly suggest that you choose licensing it because you can profit from your invention for years or even decades. For a better understanding on how you earn royalties by licensing an invention, please refer to entry #28 above (License Out Your Smart Ideas and Earn Royalties). Selling your patent is not advisable because you only profit from your invention once. But if you license it, you earn money from every unit of your invention that gets sold in the market.

Your royalty percentage depends on several factors. Such factors include the following: the novelty of the product, the quality of the patent protection, and the profitability of the product. If you think that you invention passes these factors with flying colors, then you should negotiate for a higher-than-average royalty percentage rate.

Note: For the ratings and tips for this method, please refer to the ratings and tips in the preceding chapter about licensing your smart ideas. The ratings and tips there are basically the same and applicable for this method. Inventing and patenting something boils down to whether you sell it or license it out.

Inspiration #30

"Failure defeat losers, failure inspires winners"

Robert T. Kiyosaki

Business #30

Franchise a Business

If you currently run a business which you think can be easily replicated, then franchising it is something you should consider. What makes a business franchisable? One, it should have a product or service that can be offered anywhere and for any demographic. Two, the operation of the business should be simple enough that it can be easily replicated. And three, the business must be profitable. Because what's the point in franchising a business that's losing money.

The process of franchising your business is a long and arduous one. With that said, I highly recommend that you seek the help of a franchise consultant. A single error in your application papers can cost you dearly. Errors would be minimized if there's a franchise consultant guiding your every move. Last but not the least, you should let your lawyer go over your franchising documents to ensure that everything is right and is in accordance to the law.

Franchising is a powerful strategy on how to grow your business fast. Not only that, you get to utilize the capital of your franchisees instead of putting up your own money. If the process goes well, you and your franchisees share in the earnings.

Ratings Based on Our Criteria

A. **Simplicity:**
As I said above, the process of franchising a business can be very complicated. There are many hoops that you have to go through.

4/10

B. **Passivity:**
The cash inflow from franchisees is mostly passive income.

8/10

C. **Scalability:**
Franchising is quite frankly one of the best ways to scale a business.

9/10

D. **Competitiveness:**
The franchising industry is teeming with businesses that are looking for franchisees. Expect a lot of competition along the way.

3/10

Tips For Success

- Create a document that precisely describes how your business works and how it makes money. Your potential franchisees need the exact details and guidelines on how to get their own business running.

- Hire an attorney. Getting advice from a professional is crucial during the franchising process. Even the smallest mistake can completely put a stop to the process.

- Be extremely selective when choosing franchisees for your business. It's easy to find people with capital but are they capable of running the business on their own. Your franchise business is at stake here. One bad franchisee can ruin everything.

- Take a look at the location of the new business before you award a franchise. Logistics is something that you should seriously consider especially if you are just starting to expand into franchising.

- Always be supportive of your franchisees. The success of your franchisees is also your success. Regularly have some face time with them. Call them often to see how they are doing or if they need help with the business.

- Build a brand. If you look at the most successful business franchises out there, you will see that they share something in common. All of them are maintaining their own unique brand. They have their own culture, beliefs, and attitudes toward their customers.

- Get a franchise consultant. This is a person who specializes in helping entrepreneurs go through the franchising process. A franchise consultant knows the ins and outs of the industry.

- Have a unique and exciting concept. It would be difficult to attract franchisees if your business doesn't offer something that's different from other franchises.

- Set aside a budget for continuous product and service research and development. You have to keep on improving your products and services if you want to stay sustainable and competitive.

- Be specific in setting restrictions for your franchisees. You have to make sure that every single one of your franchisees are operating within the bounds of the brand you are trying to build. It's necessary to set up specific instructions and restrictions on hiring, training, and other business practices.

Myths About Franchising

- It's impossible to fail with a franchise. Every business has the potential to fail. Despite the fact you have a set business system to follow, you still have to implement it correctly. In addition, these systems aren't perfect. Identifying where you can make improvements will ensure the franchise grows stronger.

- The franchise needs to be something I'm passionate about. This is not always the case. If you love playing tennis and think a franchise in this area is a good idea – think again!

- Buying a fast-growing franchise is a good idea. You need to think about what it's going to be like running one of these franchises and whether you'll enjoy doing it. Furthermore, a franchise that may be experiencing rapid growth may equally slow down rapidly, and by the time you've invested, it could be too late.

- A franchise is just a business in a box. You can't just expect to buy a franchise and watch it grow overnight without doing anything. You still need to apply your business skills, have a good understanding of the industry and be dedicated to effectively marketing the business.

Inspiration #31

"Expect the best. Prepare for the worst. Capitalize on what comes."

Zig Ziglar

Business #31

Retail Arbitrage on eBay

Before anything else, we need to clearly define what retail arbitrage means. In retail arbitrage, you simply buy a product from a retail store then resell it at a higher price for a profit. For example, you purchase a piece of clothing from a retail store like Target or Walmart for $10 then list it for sale on eBay for $15. If someone buys it, then you have a $5 profit. Just rinse and repeat.

Retail arbitrage on eBay simply involves purchasing products from various sources (sometimes at a great discount) then listing them for sale on eBay. You can get your products not just from retail stores. You can even purchase products from other eBay sellers then list them for sale on the site. It's basically a process of buying and selling products. To make the most out of retail arbitrage, you need to focus on a niche. Working within a specific niche makes it easier for you to attract repeat customers. They know what types of products you are selling so they are more inclined to visit your store and listings.

Ratings Based on Our Criteria

A. **Simplicity:**
   The business model is really simple. Buy products from retail stores then list them for sale at a profit on eBay.

   9/10

B. **Passivity:**
   You are directly selling products the way traditional stores do. So the income you earn is mostly direct income.

   5/10

C. **Scalability:**
   You can easily scale the business by adding more products in your eBay store.

   8/10

D. **Competitiveness:**
   Competition depends on your niche. For example, there are too many people selling books on eBay. So you might consider targeting a less competitive niche.

   4/10

Tips For Success

- Focus on selling high-quality products. Keep in mind that eBay has its own review and rating system.
- Understand the costs of selling on eBay before you jump in.
- Start the bids in the lower margins to attract bargain hunters.
- Take high-quality photos of the items you are selling.
- Timing is everything so you should schedule your listings.

- Make your product descriptions as clear and informative as possible.
- Promote PayPal as your primary payment option. Many online shoppers are wary about paying through their credit cards.
- Promote your eBay store in social media (i.e. Facebook, Twitter, and Instagram).
- Cross-promote your products within eBay.
- Have a return policy. This is great in building your brand and in nurturing loyal customers.

Myths About Retail Arbitrage

- That retail arbitrage is too competitive. Every profitable business has a certain degree of competition. To minimize that, you simply need to niche down and provide quality products that will compel customers to be loyal to your brand and become repeat customers.

- That scaling a retail arbitrage business is difficult. If you leverage the power of social media, you can bring your offers in front of your ideal customers at a cheap price. This will allow you to sell a lot more products without having to increase the number of products you sell. Of course another way to scale would be to add more to your product line.

Inspiration #32

"A goal is a dream with a deadline."

Napoleon Hill

Business #32

Create a Podcast

If you like talking to people, creating a podcast might be something that will fit perfectly into your alley. But what is a podcast? Generally speaking, it is an online version of a radio show or program. But there are a lot of significant differences between a podcast and a radio program. One, a podcast is usually self-produced which means you have to invest in your own gear from microphones, headphones, recorders, and other necessary equipment. You can record your podcast in the comforts of your home or office.

Another great feature of a podcast is that you have the ability to reach anyone in the world. Your potential audience is basically limitless. A sushi waiter in Japan and a millionaire in New York have as much the same chance to listen to you and whatever it is you are talking about in your podcast. This gives you incredible leverage. The biggest podcasters out there today can command millions of listeners per episode. For instance, Joe Rogan of the Joe Rogan Experience podcast says that his podcast gets more than 10 million downloads every episode. That's huge. We are not saying here that you should target the same figures. We are just pointing out the fact that podcasting can be lucrative if you have can build an interesting podcast.

However, the biggest advantage of creating a podcast is that you have the flexibility to talk about anything you want. Unlike in a traditional radio show wherein you have to follow the script provided by a producer or by the station itself, podcasting gives you the freedom to talk about any topic in any way you want. If you are an independent podcaster, you have full control over your podcast.

Starting a podcast is not too difficult. If you have the necessary equipment, you can start right away. The first step you should take is to sign up with an online podcasting platform. There are several companies that offer such a platform. Some are free and some have monthly subscription fees. Needless to say, the paid podcasting platforms offer better services with more features and functions. But if you don't have the budget, you can always start with the free alternatives. In fact, some successful podcasters suggest that you start with the free platforms to test the waters and gain some experience. With this strategy, you get to learn how podcasting works and how you can promote your podcast. You can learn about the ins and outs of the industry this way.

How do you make money from podcasting? There are several monetization methods that you can explore. Some podcasting platforms pay their podcasters based on various metrics. It could be per download or per listen (CPM). You can forego using a podcasting company and record and upload your podcast on your own website or blog. You earn passive income through this method by allowing ads to run on your website. These advertisements can be third-party ads from an ad program like Google Adsense or advertisements from an affiliate marketing company.

You can also earn good income from your podcast by promoting products and services in the podcast itself. For this to work, you must have a decent number of regular listeners so that businesses and brands will be willing to become sponsors. How podcast sponsorship works is quite simple. A company or brand basically pays you to mention or promote their products or services in your podcast. This can be in a per episode basis or the company can sponsor your whole program.

Ratings Based on Our Criteria

A. Simplicity:

Podcasting is really simple if you consider how easy it is to start one. All you need are the necessary equipment and a distribution platform.

8/10

B. Passivity:

Most of the money you earn from podcasting will be from sponsors that you directly plug about in your podcast. Initially, some of the income you earn will not be passive in nature since you're exchanging your time for it. However, residual earnings that continue to accrue from episodes you created in the past will be passive.

5/10

C. **Scalability:**
There is no other way to scale a podcast than to increase your viewership and acquire more sponsores. Of course, you can consider starting a completely different podcast on top of the current one but this is not advisable at all. It will just divide your time and resources.

5/10

D. **Competitiveness:**
There's very little competition in the podcasting arena. It seems that many people are not yet sold on the power of podcasting to attract an audience and create influence online.

5/10

Tips For Success

- Find your voice and stick to it. Having a unique voice is very important in podcasting. You must have a unique style in talking about your topic to separate yourself from other podcasters. Offer a different way of tackling the topics in your niche.

- Address questions from your listeners in your podcast. This is a powerful technique in encouraging your listeners to connect and interact with you. Reading and answering questions by your audience live in your podcast creates the impression that you care about them and their thoughts.

- Do not saturate your podcast with ads and sponsorships. It is understandable that you make some money from your podcast but there should be a good balance between your content and the things you are promoting. If you plug a product or service every several minutes, your listeners will get turned off.

- Invest in high-quality recording equipment. Low-quality sound will make your listeners think that you do not seem to be serious about your podcast. With that said, you should get good equipment to ensure that you deliver the best possible sound in your podcast. Having high-quality sound also means listeners can download or even repurpose your audio files without them losing their quality.

- Create a schedule and stick to it. You have to follow a schedule so that your listeners will know when to tune in. This also allows your listeners to set aside time to listen to your podcast.

- Find a niche and stick to it. If you look into the most popular podcasts today, you will quickly realize that most of them have niche topics. It's much easier to grow a loyal following if you stick to a specific niche. If it's a general podcast wherein you talk about topics from numerous sources and disciplines, listeners will just come and go. For example, there's very little incentive for a soccer fan to be listening to the next episode if he knows that you won't be talking about soccer.

- Don't alienate your listeners. As much as possible, stay away from creating controversy. Yes, controversy can easily attract a nice number of new listeners but if it's the type of controversy that can alienate a lot of your listeners, it won't benefit you in the long run.

- Collaborate with other podcasters. Look for other podcasters who are in the same niche as yours then ask them if they would be willing to collaborate with you for certain episodes. This is a great way to leverage each other's audience. It is a win-win situation for you and the other podcaster.

- Promote your podcast in social media. Use popular social networking sites like Facebook, Twitter, YouTube, and Instagram. What you do is upload bits or excerpts from your podcast to these social networking sites to give people a taste of what you are offering in your podcast.

- Reach out to potential sponsors. In this business, you should have the confidence to directly approach brands and ask them if they would be interested in sponsoring your podcast. If you have great content and a good following, brands would be more than happy to talk to you about sponsorships.

Frequently Asked Questions and Answers

- How much money can I make from a podcast?
  - There are a lot of factors that determine how much you should be earning from your podcast. The biggest factor is of course the monetization model you are using and the average number of listeners you attract per episode. The industry average is that you should be earning between $25 and $50 for 1,000 listeners. This is just a rough estimate.

- What equipment do I need to start a podcast?
  - Basically, you need the following gadgets: microphone, headphone, pop filter, boom, recording and editing software, ID3 Editor, and a camera.

- Do podcasts use a lot of data?
  - As a rule of thumb, majority of podcasts use approximately 1MB per minute. So a 40-minute podcast will consume around 40MB of data.

- How do I monetize a podcast?
  - There are several monetization methods that you can explore. These include the following: coaching, affiliate marketing, sponsored segments, courses, advertising, donations, subscriptions, premium content, events, physical products, books, public speaking, and crowdfunding.

Myths About Podcasting

- That you can't afford a home studio. When you're starting out, It's important to remember you don't need to buy the best of everything. You can easily set up a home studio that can get the job done for under $100 (provided you already have a computer)

- That you don't have the time. Finding the time to do a podcast required good time management skills but you also want to be honest with yourself about why you want to do it. If your "why" isn't strong enough, you'll struggle to find the time.

- That you don't have any radio or presenting experience. While its important to know how to use your voice, if you have a genuine passion for your content and want to share it with your listeners, the rest can be taught.

Inspiration #33

"Logic will get you from A to B. Imagination will take you everywhere."

Albert Einstein

Series #	Book Title
1	Affiliate Marketing
2	Passive Income Ideas
3	Affiliate Marketing + Passive Income Ideas (2-in-1 Bundle)
4	Facebook Advertising
5	Dropshipping
6	Dropshipping + Facebook Advertising (2-in-1 Bundle)
7	Real Estate Investing For Beginners
8	Credit Cards and Credit Repair Secrets
9	Real Estate Investing And Credit Repair Strategies (2-in-1 Bundle)
10	Passive Income Ideas With Affiliate Marketing (2nd Edition)
11	Passive Income With Dividend Investing
12	Stock Market Investing For Beginners
13	The Simple Stock Market Investing Blueprint (2-in-1 Bundle)
14	Real Estate And Stock Market Investing Mastery (3-in-1 Bundle)
15	Amazon FBA Mastery

Business #33

Start a Deals Newsletter

Before we proceed, it's important that we define what constitutes a deals newsletter. I am assuming that you are familiar with newsletters. These are online subscriptions which deliver to you messages on a certain topic or theme on a daily, weekly, or random basis. To subscribe to these services, you simply input your email address in a form and you'll start receiving messages and updates via email. A deals newsletter works exactly this way. However, the messages that are sent to you are about new deals, promos, discounts, and prizes on certain products and services.

Let's say that you are a customer looking for deals on auto parts. You come across a website that has a deals newsletter on auto parts. You input your email address and subscribe to the newsletter. With that completed, you will be receiving messages about the latest deals and discounts in auto parts in your inbox. That's basically how a deals newsletter works.

You can earn passive income by creating your own deals newsletter. Find a niche and scour the web for the latest deals, discounts, and promos relevant to the niche. Create messages about these deals and send these as a blast to those who subscribed to your deals newsletter. To create the newsletter itself, you need an email delivery service (i.e. MailChimp, Aweber etc.), which automates some of the process. To let people know about the newsletter, you should build a blog or a website that serves as the main entry point for your potential subscribers.

How do you make money from a deals newsletter? There are several monetization methods that you can explore. The top choice would be affiliate marketing. For example, look for the newest deals and promos on Amazon and inform your subscribers about these deals. If people buy products from Amazon through your referrals, you get to earn commissions. You can also do sponsored listing where businesses pay you to promote their offers to your audience.

Ratings Based on Our Criteria

A. **Simplicity:**
   Maintaining a deals newsletter requires a little bit of work because you need to constantly scour the web for the latest deals. However, you can simplify this by hiring freelancers to help you find deals, which you then promote to your audience.

   6/10

B. **Passivity:**
   When done correctly, majority of your earnings from promoting deals will be passive.

   7/10

C. **Scalability:**
   To scale the business, either you create another newsletter in another niche or you increase the amount of messages you send to subscribers.

   6/10

D. **Competitiveness:**
   There are numerous deals newsletters out there so expect tough competition.

   3/10

Tips For Success

- Build a blog or a website first before you create a deals newsletter. Use the blog to attract readers which you then entice to sign up with your newsletter.

- Focus on a niche. You are spreading yourself too thin if you target a general niche. For example, focus in iPhone deals instead of trying to find deals on all brands of smartphones.

- Use an email automation software like MailChimp or Aweber. These services charge a fee but they're worth it because they take a lot of the burden off your back.

- Don't exaggerate the deals you are promoting. If the discount in a product is 10%, don't claim that it's 12%. Lying to your subscribers is the easiest way to have them unsubscribe.

- Offer an incentive for people to subscribe. It could be a free ebook, a piece of software, a free product, etc.

- Promote your deals newsletter on social media. A quick post on Facebook or Twitter can potentially attract a few dozen subscribers if you have a decent following in your social accounts.

- Sign up with the largest affiliate marketing companies out there like Amazon, eBay, Commission Junction, ClickBank, Rakuten, etc. These are some of the places where you can find great deals, which you can then refer to your subscribers.

- Subscribe to other deals newsletters in your niche. This strategy is all about getting scoops from your competitors. It's not unethical at all. It's just business. It's similar to a TV station watching another station to get scoops on the latest news.

- Try to replicate your success with another newsletter in another niche. This doubles the amount of work you do but it's worth it because you can potentially double your income from your newsletters.

- Collaborate with other owners of newsletters. The trick here is to collaborate only with those who are in the same niche as yours. You can cross-promote each other's newsletters.

Myths About Deals Newsletters

- That operating a deals newsletter business is very time consuming. This need not be the case. When you leverage auto responders to automate the email messaging process, hire virtual assistants to scour the web for deals, subscribe to company emails to get notified when they run discount promotions etc. you can free up your time to focus on other things you love doing

- That a deals newsletter business is hard to monetize. On the contrary, there are many ways to monetize a deals newsletter business. The obvious one is via Affiliate Marketing. However, there are other ways like: sponsored listing, creating courses teaching people how to start their own deals newsletter business, consulting with businesses that want you to help them set up their own deals newsletter etc. You are only limited by how creative you're willing to get with this.

Inspiration #34

"Good ideas come from bad ideas, but only if there are enough of them."

Seth Godin

Series #	Book Title
1	Affiliate Marketing
2	Passive Income Ideas
3	Affiliate Marketing + Passive Income Ideas (2-in-1 Bundle)
4	Facebook Advertising
5	Dropshipping
6	Dropshipping + Facebook Advertising (2-in-1 Bundle)
7	Real Estate Investing For Beginners
8	Credit Cards and Credit Repair Secrets
9	Real Estate Investing And Credit Repair Strategies (2-in-1 Bundle)
10	Passive Income Ideas With Affiliate Marketing (2nd Edition)
11	Passive Income With Dividend Investing
12	Stock Market Investing For Beginners
13	The Simple Stock Market Investing Blueprint (2-in-1 Bundle)
14	Real Estate And Stock Market Investing Mastery (3-in-1 Bundle)
15	Amazon FBA Mastery

Business #34

Develop Wordpress Themes

Wordpress remains as the top content management system on the internet. Millions of websites and blogs use the platform because of its open-source management system. Needless to say, there's a huge market demand for all things related to Wordpress. These range from plugins to mobile applications. However, one of the biggest and most in-demand Wordpress-related products are Wordpress themes.

With that said, if you are a skilled and experienced web developer, you should consider creating Wordpress themes and selling them online. Thousands of developers make a full-time income from this endeavour. What's great about creating a Wordpress theme is that you can license it in the sense that people who download and use it have to pay you a fee. There's no limit to the number of people who can download and get your theme. If you create a popular theme, that's easy and recurring money going into your bank account.

Ratings Based on Our Criteria

A. **Simplicity:**
Developing Wordpress themes is not that difficult if you are a savvy web developer. Alternatively, you can hire someone to develop these themes for you.
7/10

B. **Passivity:**
Majority of the income you earn from sales of your Wordpress themes are passive in nature.
9/10

C. **Scalability:**
You can scale your earnings from the themes you created by making even more profitable themes or hiring a team of developers to create themes for you.
9/10

D. **Competitiveness:**
You will be competing with thousands of other developers who are creating Wordpress themes.
3/10

Tips For Success

- Always code according to Wordpress standards. It makes customization easier for your users.
- Always make sure that your code is up to date. Outdated code can cause a lot of problems for your users.
- Create simple and uncluttered designs. Less is more.
- Make sure that your theme is compatible with the most popular plugins within the Wordpress community.
- Make your theme compatible to translation apps and plugins.
- Always offer support to your users. This is very important considering the fact that you are commercially selling your themes.
- Regularly perform quality checks of your themes.
- Create a demo site so that potential users can test and see your theme in action.
- Create a theme with a responsive design. This means it is compatible not only with laptops and desktop computers but with smart phones and tablets as well.
- Make your theme easy to customize. Users tend to patronize themes that they can change and modify at a whim.

Myths About Developing Wordpress Themes

- The more expensive the theme, the better. Generally speaking, paid themes offer you more support, more in-depth documentation than free ones. However, it's not always the case that a $300 Wordpress theme is better than a $50 theme.

- That you have to pick a theme that looks like everything else on the market. On the contrary, it can be advantageous to be original. This will allow you to create a brand and an loyal audience

- That Wordpress themes can't be fully edited and personalized. On the contrary, Wordpress offers a variety of options to adapt the selected theme to your branding or strategy.

Inspiration #35

"What do you need to start a business? Three simple things: know your product better than anyone, know your customer, and have a burning desire to succeed."

David Thomas

Business #35

Dividend Investing

Buying stocks that pay dividends can reward you over time if you are smart with your investments. What's great about dividend-paying stocks is that they offer steady payments. This is not to mention the fact that you get the opportunity to reinvest the dividends back in the company to purchase additional shares of stock. Many dividend-paying stocks usually represent enterprises that are considered as financially mature and stable. This means that the prices of the stocks of these companies may steadily increase, giving shareholders periodic dividend payments.

Companies that pay dividends also tend to be more stable and less volatile than the market in general. With that said, they may offer lower risks compared to companies who don't pay dividends and companies who have volatile price movements. Investing in dividend-paying stocks is a great option for young people who want to generate wealth during the long haul or for older adults who want to build a steady source of income during their retirement.

A very important benefit of investing in dividend-paying stocks is the power of compounding. This refers to the practice of generating earnings then reinvesting the earnings back into the business. Dividend compounding happens when you reinvest your dividends to purchase additional shares of stock from the company.

Ratings Based on Our Criteria

A. **Simplicity:**
   You are dealing with shares of stock here so, at the very least, you should be knowledgeable of how the stock market works.

   6/10

B. **Passivity:**
   Nearly all of the money you make from dividend stocks are passive income.

   8/10

C. **Scalability:**
   To scale your earnings, you either buy more shares or use your dividends to purchase more shares or you can use both methods.

   7/10

D. **Competitiveness:**
   There's very little competition in the sense that competitors can't affect how much you earn from your dividend stocks.

   6/10

Tips For Success

- As much as possible, only invest in high-quality firms that have a proven record of growth, stability, and profitability.

- Choose which stocks to invest in by ranking them based on their dividend histories. If a company's dividend payments have steadily grown for years, then it's probably a good bet.

- Invest in companies that pay shareholders the most dividends per dollar they invest.

- Rank stocks based on their dividend yields. Look for companies who have been trading below their 10-year historical average valuation multiple.

- Don't get fooled by companies that pay out all of their income as dividends to shareholders. This may look good in the short haul but the company has no margin for safety. In short, investing in the company can be too risky.

- Invest in companies that show a history of steady growth. If a company has maintained its growth for 10 years, the company will likely maintain such growth in the coming years.

- Invest in the companies that attract people in times of panic and recessions. These companies are usually stable even during hard times.

- If you can sell your stocks for much more than their worth, you probably should take the money. Get the funds and reinvest them in companies that pay higher dividends.

- More often than not, when a company reduces its dividends, that's a red flag and you should consider options on how to cash out and exit from the company.

- Diversify, diversify, and diversify. Spreading your investments is still one of the best strategies in dividend investing.

Myths About Dividend Investing

- That dividend investing is just for retired people. Admittedly, dividend investing is very attractive for seniors, since typically their investing goals are income generation and capital preservation. However, younger investors also want the benefits from the dividend stocks, even when their portfolio value might not be as big compared to the seniors.

- That dividend investing are safe forms of investments. Investing in general is risky. There is always the possible risk that you will lose money. However, there are some investments, which include dividend stocks, which have a tendency to be safer compared to others.

Inspiration #36

"The value of an idea lies in the using of it."

Thomas Edison

Business #36

Authority Sites

Before we proceed, it's important that we clearly define what constitutes an authority site. A general definition would go this way: *"An authority site is a website that contains the most valuable content about a particular topic. The content in the site is so good that people knowledgeable in the industry often refer to it or recommend it to their less knowledgeable counterparts."* For example, let's say you want to learn about starting a social media marketing business. Of course, your first step is to find information about it. It so happens that the websites with the best content about social media marketing are Search Engine Land and Social Media Examiner. So these two websites are perfect examples of authority sites.

Here are the core characteristics of an authority website:

- It contains the best content about a particular topic. The content can be in the form of articles, videos, images, infographics, etc.
- It's often cited by people knowledgeable in the field. In our example above, Search Engine Land and Social Media Examiner are often cited by social media marketers and experts. This means that they put a lot of value and respect on the contents of the two websites.
- It has dynamic content. Dynamic content means two things. One, it is always up to date. And two, it is very easy for readers to interact with the content. They can share it and they can copy it and post it in their own digital spaces.
- It is often cited as a source by other websites. For example, if you have a website about martial arts training that is often cited as a source by hundreds of websites about martial arts, then you are an authority site on martial arts training.
- It's frequently updated with new content. In the first place, it's hard to maintain an authority site if its content remains stagnant for long periods of time. The best authority sites are the ones that are regularly updated with new information, new data, new images, and new analysis (for opinionated authority sites).

As you can see, it's not too difficult to create and build an authority site. If a website meets the criteria listed above, then it passes as an authority site. However, in order to build an authority site, you must have patience and a penchant for exhaustive research. Always remember that for you to be considered as an authority in a specific niche, you must be the best at one or many of the following: the best content, the best articles, the best photos, the best videos, the best infographics etc.

The next obvious question now is how do you earn passive income from an authority website? There are several monetization methods that you can use. Most of these methods are discussed in this book. For example, you can use affiliate marketing. You can promote affiliate products in the articles that you post in the authority site. You can also make money through advertising. You can sign up with advertising programs like Google Adsense and display their ads in your site. Or you can deal directly with businesses and companies who want to directly advertise in your website.

Or better yet, you can create your own product or service and use your authority site as your selling platform. For example, let's say that you have an authority site about learning a new language. You can monetize it by creating an ebook or a video tutorial series about tips on how to learn a new language. You can sell these items as downloadable digital products. This is just one of several product ideas that you can explore.

Ratings Based on Our Criteria

A. **Simplicity:**

Building an authority website requires a lot of your time and resources. With that said, it can't be described as a simple business model. It only gets simpler if you decide to outsource most of the content creation and website management responsibilities to online freelancers.

6/10

B. Passivity:

Building an authority website can be difficult and time-consuming but the rewards are worth it. Most of the income you earn from it becomes more and more passive in nature as time goes by.

8/10

C. Scalability:

Your success in building an authority site can be replicated by building similar websites albeit in different niches. To make your life easier, you should consider hiring freelance writers to create the content that you publish in your authority sites.

9/10

D. Competitiveness:

Competition depends on the niche you have entered. However, generally speaking, there's great competition no matter what niche you enter these days.

4/10

Tips For Success

- Focus on creating great content. High-quality content is the foundation of every authority site. Why would anyone recommend your site if you don't have valuable content? The general rule is that before you publish a piece content in your site, you should first ask yourself the following question: "Is this an article I would gladly share with friends if someone else wrote it?"

- Create content that can be understood by an Average Joe. Being clear and understandable should be your topmost goal when writing a piece. You created the site to help people understand the subject. You didn't create it to impress people with your amazing prose.

- Allow people to interact and engage with your content. You may think of yourself as an expert in the topic but there's always space for new or better ideas. Let people comment on your articles. Let them interact with each other. The more they engage in your site, the more attention your site gets.

- Pay close attention to SEO. Here's something you should be aware of. Majority of authority sites get at least 80% of their traffic from search engines. Getting most of your traffic from search engines means people are voting for your content through backlinks and citations. You can boost this even further by optimizing your content with the right keywords and phrases. If you don't know how to implement SEO, you should start learning about it now.

- Go beyond what others in your niche are doing. If a competitor is writing 1000-word articles, you should write 2000-word articles. If your competitor interviewed two experts in your niche, you should interview three or four experts. The point here is that you should strive to be always one step ahead of the competition. The moment you start lagging behind, you will slowly lose your reputation as an authority site.

- Don't over-monetize your authority site. Too much advertisements or too much sales pitches can make you look desperate. It creates the impression that you are merely in the business of making money and nothing more.

- Be honest and always stay transparent. This is very important if you run an authority site wherein you have to regularly offer your opinion on things. Honesty and transparency also means providing disclosures about the businesses, companies, and other entities that you have dealings with. For example, if a piece of content you published was sponsored by a company, you should disclose that it's a sponsored content.

- Never stop promoting your site. Be active in social media sites like Facebook, Twitter, LinkedIn, Instagram, and even Pinterest. Never stop engaging with people who might be interested in looking at your content. Run advertising campaigns if you have the budget for it. In short, just keep hustling. Self-promotion is a huge aspect of building an authority site.

- Build an email list. What you do is create a newsletter and invite visitors of your website to sign up if they want to be notified about the latest updates in your website. If you have amazing content, there's no reason why anyone should refuse to sign up with your newsletter. What's great about building an email list is that it can be automated using the right tools and resources.

- Ask your readers what they want. Are there any topics they want clarified? What should you write about next? Asking questions is a great way to brainstorm for new ideas. Hell, you should also consider asking your readers to write a guest post for your site.

Myths About Creating An Authority Site

- That people will come to your site once it's built and has quality content. That's not always the case. While having quality content on your site will attract some readers, you still need to actively promote your site on social media in order to scale it quickly.

- That it's difficult to monetize authority sites. Well, I think by now we both know that's not true. There are so many ways you can monetize your site and we have already covered much of that when we discussed ways to monetize deals sites.

Congratulations!

The sixth character of the password required to unlock the business scorecard is letter z.

Inspiration #37

"The fastest way to change yourself is to hang out with people who are already the way you want to be."

Reid Hoffman

Business #37

Membership Sites

What is a membership site? This is a website the content of which can only be accessed by registered members. It's similar to a secret online forum, only this time you have to pay a membership fee to gain access to the content. Just think of a gated and exclusive club. To gain access to the entertainment inside the club, you have to pay an entrance fee. That's basically how membership sites work. These sites are filled with valuable content, which you can only access if you register as a member and pay the relevant fees.

How do you earn passive income from a membership site? Aside from the membership fee which you can collect monthly or yearly, you can further monetize the content of the site through various methods like affiliate marketing and advertising. You can also directly sell digital products to your members. Content in membership sites can include PDF files, ebooks, video tutorials, software downloads, webinars, exclusive forums, consultancy services, exclusive chat rooms, etc.

Now to the obvious question: How do you create a membership website? If you are an experienced web developer, you can do it yourself. If you know nothing about coding, you can always hire a freelance developer to get the job done. Additionally, there are numerous tools, resources, and apps out there that you can use to create membership sites with ease. Such tools and apps include MemberPress, Wild Apricot, Digital Access Pass, SubHub, WishList Member, Easy Member Pro, MemberGate, and SiteManPro.

Ratings Based on Our Criteria

A. **Simplicity:**
   Building and maintaining a membership site requires a lot of work. This can be a full-time job especially if the site has a membership count that is in the thousands.
   5/10

B. **Passivity:**
   The recurring subscription income you earn may be passive but you have to take into account the immense amount of time and effort that you put into the business. Of course, to make this even more passive, some of the day-to-day management of the site can be outsourced to a virtual assistant manager.
   6/10

C. **Scalability:**
   To scale the business, create another membership website.
   7/10

D. **Competitiveness:**
   There seems to be a membership site for every conceivable topic these days.
   3/10

Tips For Success

- Take the time to research for a less competitive niche. You have a better chance of achieving success if there aren't already dozens of membership sites in the niche you want to enter.

- Learn from the best. Check out the services of popular membership sites like Copyblogger, eDiets, and E-Course Lunch Formula.

- Decide on the type of content you will put in your membership site before you start building it. It's easier to build the site if you know what's going to be published in it.

- Use tools and apps to make it easier and quicker to build your membership site. We've mentioned some of these tools and apps above (i.e. MemberPress, Wild Apricot, Digital Access Pass, SubHub, etc.)

- Consider offering a free trial period for new members. This is one of the most effective strategies in attracting new sign-ups for membership sites.

- Offer a combination of free and paid content in your membership site. This means that all of your members will find something of value in the site.

- Regularly update and improve the content of your website. If it remains stagnant for too long, that's when people will start cancelling their memberships.

- Offer a variety of content in your site. Variety translates to enhanced engagement from your members. Put out ebooks, video courses, webinars, podcasts, online conferences, and Q & As. The more, the better.

- Create a forum inside the site where all members can interact with each other. Building a forum is very effective in encouraging members to be more active in the site.

- Regularly offer deals, discounts, promos, and contests to reward your members. They'll appreciate your efforts and give them even more reasons to stick around.

Myths About Membership Sites

- That membership sites are easy money. Sure, membership sites can be a fantastic business to run as your recurring income builds month on month; however that doesn't mean it's easy. Unlike other forms of information products where the customer journey concludes with a purchase; with membership sites that's when your customer journey starts, and your responsibility is to continuously deliver a product that they'll pay for on an ongoing basis.

- That membership sites are difficult to set up. This may be the case if you're not a web developer. However, in these day and age, this should not stop you. You can learn the basic skills required to build a membership site. Alternatively, you can outsource this process to a freelance web developer from upwork.com or fiverr.com

- That you need to have all your content ready. This is not always the case. If your membership offers live training, ongoing coaching or is primarily community based, then your product isn't pre-created, static content – it's content that is produced in real-time; so until you have members onboard you're not actually creating any content at all.

Inspiration #38

"There are no secrets to success. It is the result of preparation, hard work, and learning from failure."

Colin Powell

Business #38

Putting Money into High-Yield Savings Accounts

A high-yield savings account is a bank account that earns you a much higher interest rate compared to a traditional savings account. Because of the higher interest rates, these accounts are also sometimes referred to as high-interest rate savings account. A traditional savings account usually yields less than 1% interest rate. High-yield savings accounts have rates that are between 1% and 4%. The difference in rates is quite substantial. Converted to cash, that's real passive income going into your bank account.

You might be asking: How can banks afford such high interest rates for deposits? Well, there's a catch for the bank when you put your money in high-yield savings accounts. For instance, you may have to pay monthly maintenance fees. There may be additional requirements to maintain a minimum balance. Banks also have to protect their interests. However, if you take into account these additional fees and requirements, they don't completely cancel out the extra earnings you generate from your high-yield savings account.

It's worth mentioning here that a lot of the banks offering high-yield savings accounts are internet banks (i.e. Synchrony, Ally, iGoBanking). The main reason internet banks can offer much higher interest rates is because they don't have the burden of spending money on physical branches and on hiring new people.

Ratings Based on Our Criteria

A. **Simplicity:**
   The process of putting money in a bank is in itself very easy. The hard part lies in finding the types of accounts that will earn you the most returns.
   8/10

B. **Passivity:**
   The additional interest you earn from high-yield savings accounts are mostly passive income.
   9/10

C. **Scalability:**
   To scale, either you put more money into your account or you open more accounts in other banks.
   6/10

D. **Competitiveness:**
   You are not competing with anyone when you open a high-yield savings account.
   10/10

Tips For Success

1. Always make sure that your high-yield savings account is covered by either the Federal Deposit Insurance Corporation or the National Credit Union Administration.

2. Try to look for an account that doesn't come with additional fees. The high interest rate means nothing if it's cancelled out by the additional fees.

3. Verify if the bank's high-yield savings accounts are truly worth it. To do this, you should read reviews and comments by people who have availed themselves of the accounts.

4. Find out about minimum balance requirements. If you don't meet the minimum balance, you will be charged a fee.

5. Ask if there's a required initial deposit. The general rule is that you should look for banks that offer lower required initial deposits.

6. Don't be fooled by teaser rates. These are rates that banks often advertise for their high-yield savings accounts. Sometimes, these rates are for a particular promo period only which means they only last for a while.

7. Take your time to shop around to look for the best deals.

8. Try internet banks. A lot of internet banks can offer high-yield savings accounts because they don't deal with high overhead costs.

9. Seek the advice of a financial consultant. It's always a good idea to seek recommendations from people knowledgeable about savings accounts.

10. Only put your money in stable and healthy banks. You will deal with less risks.

Inspiration #39

"Don't worry about failure; you only have to be right once."

Drew Houston

Business #39

Rent Out Your Car

Do you have a car that you don't drive most days? Instead of letting it sit idle, why not earn some money by renting it out? This is a business model that several companies have explored in recent years. The business model is straightforward. You sign up with the company, complete your profile, and then create a listing for your car. Your listing should include pertinent information such as the model of your car, its age, when it's available, and how much you charge per hour. Include inside and outside photos of your car. Communication between you and the interested renter depends on the system put forth by the company.

Basically, the set up here is that you list your car in the website and if someone is interested in renting it out, you'll get an alert or a notification. You then talk about how and where the renter can pick up your car. Of course, as the middleman in the transaction, the company gets a percentage cut from your earnings. That's how they make money on their end.

There are several companies that already offer this service. These companies include Turo, GetAround, RelayRides, JustShareIt, and Spride. Although they offer the same service, these companies differ from each other with regards to the way they manage transactions between car owners and renters. You should take the time to review each company's business processes so that you can choose the one appropriate for you.

Ratings Based on Our Criteria

A. **Simplicity:**
The business is very simple. Just sign up with the company offering the service then create a listing for your car.
9/10

B. **Passivity:**
Most of the income you earn are passive income.
8/10

C. **Scalability:**
To scale, you probably need to buy another car but that may not be economically viable.
5/10

D. **Competitiveness:**
This business model hasn't really caught on so you don't have to worry much about competition.
5/10

Tips For Success

- Choose the right company. So far, the biggest names in the industry are HyreCar, Turo, Drivy, GetAround, and GoGet. Make sure that any of these companies are available in your location before you sign up.

- Make your listing as descriptive as possible. Include important information like the model of the car, the brand, the color, etc. If there are any problems with the car, include the information in your description as well.

- Thoroughly clean your car before you offer it for rent. Nobody wants to rent a dirty and smelly car.

- Post high-quality photos of the car. People judge cars by how they look. If all you have is a grainy photo, no one will bite into your listing.
- Make sure that the car is working perfectly before you list it to avoid unnecessary problems with both the company and the renters.
- Give utmost focus to marketing

Inspiration #40

"Our greatest weakness lies in giving up. The most certain way to succeed is always to try just one more time."

Thomas Edison

Business #40

Rent Out Your Clothes

Check out your closet. Are there clothes there in perfect condition that you don't regularly use? What if I told you that you can take them out, offer them for rent to strangers, and earn some extra cash on the side? It's true. There are businesses today that allow you to rent out your unused clothes to complete strangers. Think of these companies as the AirBnb of fashion. Such companies include Glam Corner, Her Wardrobe, The Volte, Designerex, Girl Meets Dress, and Hire My Clothes. Although these businesses have their differences, their business model is similar. They serve as the middlemen between people who have clothes to rent out and those looking to rent them.

For example, let's say you have a lot of clothes that you want to rent out for cash. You sign up with Glam Corner. You take pictures of your unused clothes, upload them on the site, put a rental price on them, and click "create listing". A person wants to rent one of the dresses so she messages you to ask further questions. The customer eventually rents your dress and completes the transaction. To deliver the dress, you either meet up with the client or ship the dress to her residence. That's basically it.

Ratings Based on Our Criteria

A. **Simplicity:**
   The business model is very simple. Sign up, list your clothes, and wait for customers.

   9/10

B. **Passivity:**
   You are receiving rental income and you're not actively exchanging your time for it so it's mostly passive income.

   9/10

C. **Scalability:**
   To scale, just add more clothes into your inventory and listings.

   8/10

D. **Competitiveness:**
   People tend to be squeamish in renting out their clothes to strangers so not many people are doing it. That means less competition for you.

   5/10

Tips For Success

- Provide as much detail in your listing as possible. This is especially important if you are renting out women's clothes. Women naturally ask a lot of questions. You can save a lot of time by describing the piece of clothing in detail.

- Make sure that all of your items are in good to excellent condition. Even the smallest tear can disappoint a customer.

- Price your items reasonably. Generally speaking, your rental price should largely depend on the cost of purchasing the clothing.

- Lingerie and swimwear are a big no-no in clothing rental services. You know why.

- Only list your best-looking clothes. Just because you have 50 unused dresses doesn't mean you should list all of them. You have to think if there's a demand for them before you put them up for rent. Too many listings can clutter your profile.

Inspiration #41

"Don't play games that you don't understand, even if you see lots of other people making money from them."

Tony Hsieh

Business #41

Rent Out Your Bike

Got a bike that you don't use too often? You should consider renting it out to make some extra cash. I'm not talking about knocking on your neighbor's door and asking if he would like to rent your bike. I'm talking about signing up with a legitimate online company that allows you to list your bike for rent. One of the pioneers of this business model is Spinlister. The company allows you to list your bike on the site. Anyone interested in renting your bike simply books it. You and the renter then talk on how and where he can pick up the bike.

There are several other companies that offer a similar bike rental service. These companies include Bike Sharing World, Bike Share, Travelling Two, Freewheeling France, Bike Bandit, and Liquid. These companies may have differences in their terms of agreement with clients or in the way they manage their business but they follow a similar business model. They all serve as a platform where you can list your bike for rent.

Ratings Based on Our Criteria

A. **Simplicity:**
   Signing up with a bike rental company is easy and hassle-free.
   8/10

B. **Passivity:**
   Most of the money you earn are passive income.
   8/10

C. **Scalability:**
   To scale, you need to put more bikes to rent out.
   6/10

D. **Competitiveness:**
   Competition can be tough in highly populated and urban areas.
   4/10

Tips For Success

- Try including accessories in the deal to entice renters. For example, a helmet or a bike light can come with the bike.
- Make your listing as descriptive as possible. Include important information like the model of the bike, the brand, the color, etc. If there are any problems with the bike, include the information in your description as well.
- Thoroughly clean your bike before you offer it for rent. Nobody wants to rent a dirty bike.
- Post high-quality photos of the bike. People judge bikes by how they look. If all you have is a grainy image of your bike, no one will be interested in renting it.
- Make sure that the bike is in perfect working condition before you list it to avoid unnecessary problems with both the company and the renters.

Business #42

Rent Out Your Garage or Parking Spot

In your neighborhood alone, chances are there's a lot of people looking for empty spaces to park their cars. Either they don't have a garage or they have one but it's not enough for their vehicles. There are two ways on how you can make money from people's parking problems. You can directly deal with the people and charge them rent by the hour or per month depending on how often they intend to use your empty garage or parking spot.

The second option is to use a company or business that connects you with people looking for garages and parking spots to rent. A good example of these companies is JustPark. This company allows you to create listings on their site advertising your empty garage or parking space. You determine how much you want to charge for your garage. Other companies with similar services include Share My Park, Elparking, and Your Parking Space.

There are also a ton of mobile apps that offer similar services. These apps include Parqex, CurbFlip, ParkingCupid, Spothero, ParkingSpotter, Spacer, SpotOn, Pavemint, Park Easier, and Rover.

Ratings Based on Our Criteria

A. **Simplicity:**
All you have to do is list your empty garage or parking space in any of the sites and apps mentioned above.
8/10

B. **Passivity:**
Most of the money you earn from this is passive income.
9/10

C. **Scalability:**
To scale this side business, you need more empty garages and parking spaces.
5/10

D. **Competitiveness:**
Most of these services haven't really caught on with the public so there's not much competition to worry you.
5/10

Tips For Success

- List your empty garage or parking spot in more than one site.
- The description of your spot is crucial. That said, list as many specifics as you can about your parking spot.
- Find sites that allow you to update your spot's availability quickly so you don't miss out on potential renters.
- Promote your spot in social media sites like Facebook and Instagram. Always remember that this is a localized business which means most of your clients will be people within your neighborhood.
- Put restrictions on what renters can park in your parking spot. If you don't have any restrictions, some renters might turn your garage into a storage facility instead of just a parking spot.

Inspiration #43

"Ideas are easy. Implementation is hard."

Guy Kawasaki

Series #	Book Title
1	Affiliate Marketing
2	Passive Income Ideas
3	Affiliate Marketing + Passive Income Ideas (2-in-1 Bundle)
4	Facebook Advertising
5	Dropshipping
6	Dropshipping + Facebook Advertising (2-in-1 Bundle)
7	Real Estate Investing For Beginners
8	Credit Cards and Credit Repair Secrets
9	Real Estate Investing And Credit Repair Strategies (2-in-1 Bundle)
10	Passive Income Ideas With Affiliate Marketing (2nd Edition)
11	Passive Income With Dividend Investing
12	Stock Market Investing For Beginners
13	The Simple Stock Market Investing Blueprint (2-in-1 Bundle)
14	Real Estate And Stock Market Investing Mastery (3-in-1 Bundle)
15	Amazon FBA Mastery

Business #43

Get Paid to Watch Videos and TV

If you spend a lot of your time watching videos online, why not try to make money from it. There are actually several companies out there that will pay you just to watch videos and TV. Most of the time you will have to register with an app or sign up with a website where you get access to videos and television programs which you can watch and be compensated for your time in watching them. Below is a quick overview of some of these companies and apps:

- **Viggle App** – This is an app designed for both iOS and Android smartphones. After downloading the app, you get access to a list of videos and television programs which you can watch. You get one point for every minute of time you spend watching the shows. As the points accumulate, you can either encash them or use them to purchase products online.

- **Swagbucks** – You earn bucks by watching videos that range from world news reports, sports highlights, to funny animal videos. You can also earn bucks by taking online surveys and surfing the web. You can redeem your earning through PayPal or exchange them for gift cards.

- **Inbox Dollars** – This is a nice alternative to Swagbucks. Aside from watching videos, Inbox Dollars also pay you to complete surveys, play online games, sign up for promotional offers, and perform web searches.

- **Perk.Tv** – This is a sister site to Viggle. You earn points by watching trending videos, watching movie trailers, answering pop quizzes, shopping online, and downloading new apps.

- **HitBliss** – This service is unique in the sense that you get paid by watching mostly commercial advertisements. The platform even allows you to watch ads using multiple devices.

- **PaidtYouTube** – As the name of the company implies, you earn money by simply watching the YouTube videos that are featured in their site.

These are just some just of the apps and companies that pay you to watch videos and television shows. Other apps and companies that you might want to check out include National Consumer Panel, Slidejoy, Success Bux, Quikrewards, AppNana, Adfun, and SendEarnings.

Ratings Based on Our Criteria

A. **Simplicity:**
   All you have to do is sign up and start watching videos.
   9/10

B. **Passivity:**
   You can watch the videos anytime you want.
   8/10

C. **Scalability:**
   To scale your earnings, you need to sign up with as many apps and companies as you can.
   6/10

D. **Competitiveness:**

There's actually very little competition in this field.

5/10

Tips For Success

- Sign up with as many apps as you can manage. More apps means more earnings and rewards.
- Try using multiple devices if you are allowed to do so. Some apps allow you to sign in simultaneously with more than one devices.
- Always bring your smartphone with you so you can watch just videos whenever you can.
- Provide your login details to people you know and trust so they can watch videos using the app as well.
- Refer the app to people you know. Most get-paid-to-watch apps have a referral program wherein you earn points for your referrals.
- Focus on the apps that bring you the most money.
- Subscribe to the newsletters of the app or company. You'll get notifications when there are new videos to watch or new surveys to answer.
- Follow the social media accounts of the app. You get updates about the latest happenings in the app.
- Make sure that you have a PayPal account. This is the most common payment method for get-paid-to-watch apps.
- Log into the app daily. The more videos you watch, the more money and rewards you earn.

Inspiration #44

"I got lucky because I never gave up the search. Are you quitting too soon? Or, are you willing to pursue luck with a vengeance?"

Jill Konrath

Business #44

Vending Machines

Running a vending machine business may look simple but starting it requires planning and hard work. First of all, you need to decide on the machine type and what type of product it dispenses. The most popular and obviously most profitable vending machines are the ones that sell drinks and snacks. This doesn't mean that these are the vending machine types that you should pursue. You can try machines that sells specific products like coffee, popcorn, cigarettes, candies, ice cream, etc. Also keep in mind that some machines dispense individual items while other machines dispense these items in bulk.

In some states in the United States, you need a permit to start operating vending machines. So make sure that you have all the proper licenses before you start installing vending machines in your preferred locations. As to the machines themselves, there are a lot of these in the market that you can purchase. They are ready-made so all you have to do is stock them with the products they were designed to dispense. It's advisable that you get in touch with a supplier who can provide you with more machines should you decide to expand your locations.

Ratings Based on Our Criteria

A. **Simplicity:**
The process of starting a vending machine business needs a bit of work but once you're established, there much less work to do.

6/10

B. **Passivity:**
It's passive income but you have to take into account the costs you incur in purchasing supplies and in restocking the machines.

6/10

C. **Scalability:**
To scale, just add more machines in more strategic locations.

8/10

D. **Competitiveness:**
The vending machine industry is actually very competitive. Most shopping malls have them.

4/10

Tips For Success

- Shop around for the best suppliers of vending machines. Only get those machines with a proven track record. Machines that break down too easily will eat away at your earnings.
- Location, location, and location. The general rule is that you should install your vending machines in places that get a lot of foot traffic.
- Vend the appropriate products in the appropriate places. It would be senseless to install a soda vending machine in an organic food store.
- Offer prompt customer service to the establishments where you install your machines.
- Only deal with reliable suppliers. Make sure that these suppliers are directly connected to the manufacturers of the machines.
- Always see to it that your machines are restocked. You might need to hire someone who makes the rounds and see if all the machines are stocked and working properly.

- Buy into a franchise. There are vending machine franchises out there that you can consider. What's good about this strategy is that you are using as leverage an already established business.
- Test out products to see which ones sell well and which don't.
- Keep your machines clean.
- Provide your contact information for the location of your machines so you can be contacted when issues arise.

Myths About Vending Business

- Running a vending business is easy and requires little effort. That's not always the case. While it is possible to make money with vending as a business, it also takes a good strategic plan as well as hard work on your especially in the beginning. Keeping the machines stocked is your number one key to making sure you have continual sales.

- The vending machine business is a hands-off business. Not many people understand the level of maintenance that goes into keeping a vending machine in tip-top shape. Let's face it, people that use your vending machines are not going to be gentle, after all, it is not theirs, so many people will be rough with it. They are electronic and these parts can and do wear out.

- You cannot make a full-time income with a vending machine business. This has been a myth that arose when many people went into the business and purchased too many machines too fast. It is wise to begin with one vending machine, once you start making money with that then look to purchase another. This way you start slow and gradually scale up as your cash flow grows.

Inspiration #45

"You gain strength, courage, and confidence by every experience in which you really stop to look fear in the face. You are able to say to yourself, I lived through this horror. I can take the next thing that comes along. You must do the thing you think you cannot do."

Eleanor Roosevelt

Business #45

Storage Rentals

Owning a self-storage facility is a profitable investment especially today wherein people tend to accumulate stuff that they barely need. More and more people are looking for spaces where they can store their belongings. According to Forbes magazine, the average profit margin for self-storage units and mini-warehouses is 11 percent. This makes them among the most profitable types of small businesses in the United States.

There are so many ways on how you can monetize a storage facility. Some of these ways are as follows:

1. Charge rents
2. Offer tenant insurance
3. Hold auctions
4. Create auxiliary sales opportunities
5. Partner with U-Haul
6. Set up vehicle storage
7. Add vending machines
8. Rent billboard space
9. Offer mail boxes

Needless to say, if you own idle land or space, you should consider building a storage facility over it. There are so many ways on how you can create a revenue stream from it. Although the initial capital needed is substantial, the maintenance cost isn't. Your main expenses will be on security and utilities. Everything else can be considered as miscellaneous expenses.

Ratings Based on Our Criteria

A. **Simplicity:**
   Starting, running, and maintaining a storage facility can be difficult and complicated.
   6/10

B. **Passivity:**
   A good portion of the money you earn from operating a storage facility are passive income.
   6/10

C. **Scalability:**
   To scale, you need to add more storage rooms or build yet another facility in a separate location.
   8/10

D. **Competitiveness:**
   As I said earlier, with more people looking for storage spaces, more entrepreneurs are also starting storage businesses.
   4/10

Tips For Success

- Offer several levels of security for your clients. Hire security guards. Put up CCTV cameras. Do everything to assure the safety of all the items stored in your facility.
- Train your staff. Train them on how to handle clients, how to handle stored items, and how to handle disasters.

- Create an atmosphere of accountability within your operation.
- Advertise your business in local papers, television stations, and radio stations.
- Set up an online marketing plan that targets people in your area.
- Offer insurance options to increase level of customer service and satisfaction.
- Set up a website where potential customers can find all the information they need about your business and your services.
- Enter into partnerships with other local businesses. Offer them affordable rates in storing their wares and products.
- Offer discounts for your most loyal customers.
- Allow potential clients to visit, tour, and check out your storage facility.

Inspiration #46

"The only thing worse than starting something and failing… is not starting something."

Seth Godin

Business #46

Licensing Music

If you have the chops for creating music, you can earn a good amount of passive income by licensing your songs and tracks. You don't have to be Ed Sheeran or Christina Aguilera to make a comfortable living from your music. In this case, we are talking about stock music licensing.

Stock music licensing is very similar to stock photography. The business model is exactly the same. You create the music, license it, and offer it royalty-free for anyone willing to use it. You make money by charging those who are going to use it. The good thing about this business model is that you still own the rights to your music and songs. People or businesses are simply paying you for the privilege of using them in their own content.

Ratings Based on Our Criteria

A. **Simplicity:**
   Although the process of creating music is complicated, selling it through licensing is quite simple.
   7/10

B. **Passivity:**
   After licensing your music, majority of the income that comes your way is passive.
   8/10

C. **Scalability:**
   If you are a prolific music composer, you can have dozens or even hundreds of tracks licensed.
   9/10

D. **Competitiveness:**
   Music licensing can be considered a saturated industry because of the heavy competition.
   4/10

Tips For Success

- Get the levels and formats right. Make sure that your tracks are of the highest quality possible.
- Only submit the best of your music for licensing especially if you are still trying to get some footing in the industry.
- When sending your work, include everything that a music supervisor needs to know about your tracks.
- Build networks and relationships with relevant and influential people in the industry.
- Be patient. It takes time for people and music supervisors to notice the quality of your work.
- Always act professionally when dealing with people in the industry. Don't let your ego get the better of you.
- Always stay in touch with former clients. They might need more of your music down the road.
- Always keep copies and files of your work.
- Set up a website where people can hear samples of your work.
- Never forget to include metadata in your music files. This will help with search engine optimization

Business #47

Network Marketing

Network marketing has earned a lot of bad press lately because of the unethical and often unscrupulous practices of some of those engaged in the business. However, you should understand that network marketing is in itself a good business opportunity if done right and with high-quality products and services. To be successful in network marketing, you have to be smart in choosing the companies you invest your money in. Don't be blinded by promises of luxury cars and instant riches. You should also familiarize yourself with the tactics of unethical network marketers to make sure that you don't ever fall into one of their traps.

Under network marketing, there are several business models that companies use. But all these models boil down to one or two systems. One, you have to grow your network. And two, you should be able to move products through your network. If you can master these two things, then network marketing is the perfect opportunity for you. Again, I have to remind you that the business models that network marketing companies use vary from company to company. It's important that you read and understand the company's business model before you even think of signing up.

In network marketing, you need to understand a variety of concepts like referrals, downlines, and uplines. It's important that you read the company's business blueprint to understand how they define these terms in the context of their business model. The term referral in one company may have a slightly different connotation in another company.

Top Network Marketing Companies Today Based On Annual Revenue

- Amway
- Avon
- Herbalife
- Vorwerk
- Mary Kay
- Infinitus
- Perfect
- Quanjian
- Natura
- Tupperware
- Nu Skin
- Primerica
- Joymain
- Jeunesse
- Oriflame
- Ambit Energy
- New Era
- USANA
- Young Living
- WorldVentures

This list is not exhaustive. There are dozens of other network marketing companies out there that register annual sales that range in the millions. Needless to say, there's money to be made in network marketing. The sheer amount of sales that these companies make every year is just astounding. Obviously, you have a lot of choices. So before you jump into any of them, you should take the time to do your research and weigh your options. The general rule is that you should choose the companies whose products you are actually interested in and you use yourself. It would be easier to sell them and you would be more comfortable pitching them to people you know.

Ratings Based on Our Criteria

A. **Simplicity:**
The business models being used by network marketing companies may look simple but they are actually complicated once you start implementing them. You have to learn how to crunch numbers. You have to learn how to compute if the money you are pulling out is more than the money you are putting into the business.

7/10

B. **Passivity:**
What's great about network marketing is that the income you earn become more and more passive as you grow your network. More people in your network means more passive income going to your bank account.

7/10

C. **Scalability:**
For sure, you can quickly scale your network marketing earnings by joining another company and applying the methods that helped you become successful in the other company.

7/10

D. **Competitiveness:**
In network marketing, competition is really tough. You must learn how to be patient. Keep in mind that there are thousands of other marketers out there offering the same products and opportunities as you. So you should be creative and smart in your approach. The main question is: "How do you differentiate yourself from the others?"

2/10

Tips For Success

- Be genuine and ethical. There's so much negativity going on in the network marketing industry right now so a lot of people are wary of joining. That said, you need to play your cards right and focus on helping people understand the positive aspects of network marketing.

- Don't fake it. This is very important considering the fact that the industry is about building networks of people who trust each other. Don't tell someone that you are earning $1000 a month if you are earning only half of that amount. Don't tell people that you bought a car with your network marketing earnings if it's not true. Please refer to tip #1. Always be genuine and ethical.

- Leverage the power of social media. Social networking sites like Facebook, Twitter, Instagram, and LinkedIn are great platforms for promoting your business. These sites have a user base that is more than a billion members. They are free to use so there's absolutely no reason why you shouldn't take advantage of them.

- Make the business about your network and not about you. The business is about connecting with people and convincing them to be part of your network. This is very hard to do if all you talk about is you. You have to show people that the business is about themselves. That it's about creating better lives for them and their loved ones.

- Find a company with products that you actually love. Here's something you should understand. It's a lot easier to sell something that you love than something that you have zero interest in.

- Don't be too aggressive with your marketing tactics. Being too aggressive and intrusive are two of the biggest reasons why network marketing is getting a lot of flak from critics. Take the time to explain to people what the business is all about before you start with your sales pitch. Don't make the impression that you are desperate.

- Understand your target market and where they are coming from. This is very important if you do most of your marketing and recruiting online. You have to be aware what types of people are more likely to sign up with your business. You have to be aware of where they usually hang out online.

- Set up your own blog or website. This should be a mandatory strategy for online network marketers. Creating your own website and blog can do wonders for your business. You can use it to attract search engine traffic, which you then try to convert into paying clients. You can also use it to build your personal brand. If you have a personal brand, people are more willing to trust you and your business offers.

- Always stay in touch with the people in your network and help them out whenever you can. This is very important especially if you are among those on top of the network. Always keep in mind that in network marketing, the success of the group is also your success as an individual.

- Have patience. If you don't have patience, network marketing can easily burn you out. That's not an exaggeration. Don't go into the business thinking that you are going to get rich quick. Just like any kind of business, achieving success in network marketing requires hard work and a lot of patience.

Frequently Asked Questions and Answers

- Isn't network marketing a pyramid scheme?
  - To be honest, some businesses out there that proclaim themselves as network marketing companies are actually operating a pyramid scheme. But you shouldn't let this discourage you. There are dozens of legitimate network marketing companies out there. This is why we always advice you to research deeply about a company before you join it.

- Do I have to know a lot of people to earn money from network marketing?
  - No. Of course, it helps if you know many people but majority of the income you are going to earn will come from people you don't personally know. Network marketing isn't about how many people you know. Instead, it's about how good you are in getting people to understand and join your business network.

- Is network marketing a stable and sustainable business opportunity?
  - In technical terms, yes. If the product or service is good then there will always be a market demanding for it. This is why you should only go with network marketing companies that have a good reputation and a line of products that are in demand.

- How much will it cost me to get started in network marketing?
  - It depends on the network marketing company you are joining. The membership package can be worth $50 or $100 or $10,000.

- Is network marketing a passing fad?
  - Network marketing has been around for more than a century. There's absolutely no reason to believe that it will ever go away. Not in the immediate future, that's for sure.

- Do I need training to get involved in network marketing?
  - A good training will always be valuable before you get started. However, it's often not necessary. Most of the time, all you need is an orientation to introduce you to the business, the business model, the products or services, and what you need to do to make money.

- How much money can I earn from network marketing?
  - It can be a few hundred dollars a month. It could also be several thousand dollars a week. The point here is that the amount you earn depends on the nature of the company you joined and the amount of hard work you put into the business.

- What types of products are sold through network marketing?
  - I'm pretty sure that you already have an idea about the types of goods being sold in the industry. To refresh your memory, the most common products in the industry include nutrition products, health care products, consumer durables, and cosmetics.

- Can I join several network marketing companies at once?
  - Yes, of course. No one is stopping you from joining as many companies as you like as long as this doesn't break any of the terms of agreement of any of the companies you joined.

- Can I work on network marketing part-time?
  - Yes. This is one of the good attributes of network marketing. Your time can be very flexible. You can work any time you want. You can work a full-time job during weekdays and pursue your network marketing business during the weekends.

Inspiration #48

"Stay self-funded as long as possible."

Garrett Camp

Business #48

Cashback Reward Cards

Most credit card companies offer a cashback reward program where a percentage of the amount people spend on their cards are paid back to them. Credit card companies offer these programs to encourage card holders to use their cards for shopping more often. Rebate percentages often range between 0.5% and 2% of the net expenditures of card holders. Needless to say, taking advantage of these programs benefits you in two main ways. One, you get discounts from products and services you purchase albeit these discounts are deferred. Two, the money going back to your card can be considered as passive income.

Credit card companies are able to pay cash back to card holders because merchants often pay an interchange fee on transactions made through a credit card. For example, when you purchase a television set with your card for $100, only $97 goes to the merchant. The difference of $3 is where the rebates and cashbacks will come from. Not all of it but a percentage of it.

Ratings Based on Our Criteria

A. **Simplicity:**
It's simple in the sense that it doesn't require a lot of work from you.
8/10

B. **Passivity:**
The rebates and cashbacks you receive are basically passive income.
8/10

C. **Scalability:**
To scale the rebates, you need to purchase more using your credit card.
5/10

D. **Competitiveness:**
It's your credit card. You can use it any way you want. There's no competition whatsoever.
10/10

Tips For Success

- Align rewards with your interests and goals. For example, if travelling is your thing, you should get a rewards card for airline miles.

- Make sure that the products and services you are purchasing are covered by your rewards card. Keep in mind that there are always exemptions.

- Pay attention to the annual fees because cards with the highest rewards often collect the highest annual fees.

- Skip cards with excess restrictions. An excess restriction means you can no longer earn rewards when you reach a certain amount of purchases.

- Look for sign-up bonuses. A sign-up bonus basically means free money.

- Use multiple cards if possible. More rewards cards means you have access to more products and services that have cashbacks.
- Take advantage of bonus offers if these are offered by your credit card provider.
- Make your purchases through online shopping malls because these often have partnerships with credit card providers.
- Make the most of bill pay options. Use your credit card to pay for your bills if you get rebates on your payments.
- Keep your spending in check. Getting more rebates doesn't always mean you are saving or earning money.

Inspiration #49

"When I'm old and dying, I plan to look back on my life and say 'wow, that was an adventure,' not 'wow, I sure felt safe.'"

Tom Preston-Werner

Business #49

Cashback Sites

A cashback website is basically a reward website that compensates its members by giving them a cut of the money it earned from goods and services that their members purchased through the site's affiliate links. Buying goods and services through a cashback site is called cashback shopping. Technically speaking, you are mostly saving money instead of making money when you use a cashback site. However, some cashback sites offer other services where you can earn some income. Such services may include online surveys and crowdsourcing tasks.

To illustrate how cashback sites operate, I'm going to provide you with a quick example. You sign up with a cashback site and use the site's affiliate links whenever you buy a product online. As you buy more products through the site's affiliate links, your points accumulate. During payday, your points are converted into rewards that you can claim. Cashback sites reward their members using various payment methods. You can be paid in cash (via PayPal, bank transfer, bank check), discounts in other products, or in gift vouchers.

Ratings Based on Our Criteria

A. **Simplicity:**
   You simply sign up with the cashback site and use their affiliate links when you go online shopping.
   9/10

B. **Passivity:**
   Aside from saving some money, you get reimbursed for some of your purchases which can be considered as passive income.
   7/10

C. **Scalability:**
   To scale your earnings, you need to join as many cashback sites as you can.
   6/10

D. **Competitiveness:**
   More members in a cashback site don't necessarily mean there's more competition.
   7/10

Tips For Success

- Join several cashback sites at a time.

- Regularly clear your computer's cookies. Most cashback sites verify if you have arrived at an online store through their site or through another website. Not clearing your cookies can cause tracking problems.

- Transfer your money as soon as you reach the minimum payout.

- Refer your friends to the cashback sites that you are using. In fact, many people make more money from their referrals compared to what they get as cashbacks.

- Never use incognito mode when using cashback sites. Incognito mode can mess up how your purchases are tracked and recorded.

- Read the details on the store to make sure that the items you are purchasing qualify for a cashback.
- Don't surf other websites while shopping online because you might override your cookies without knowing it.
- Add items to your shopping cart and check out immediately after adding the items. This is to make sure that the cashback site recorded your purchases.
- Turn off ad blockers in your browser. Again, these blockers can mess with the cashback site's tracking system.
- If you have several browser windows open, see to it that you make your purchase on the shopping site from the window that was opened through the rebate website.

Inspiration #50

"Success is the sum of small efforts – repeated day in and day out."

Robert Collier

Business #50

Refinance Your Mortgage

I know exactly what you are thinking right now. Can I really earn passive income by refinancing my mortgage? Oh yes, you sure can. Let me explain in brief how this works. Let us say for instance that you are making monthly mortgage payments of $1,500 for your home in the moment. Now, let us say that you can reduce that monthly payment from $1,500 to $1,300 a month through mortgage refinancing. That basically means you will be pocketing the difference of $200 every month. It may not be much but $200 is $200. Technically speaking, that amount can be considered as passive income.

At this point, you might be saying: "But mortgage refinancing isn't free. You have to pay for and settle the closing costs." Yes, you are absolutely right. This is why refinancing your mortgage as a source of passive income only applies to certain situations. If you are planning to live in your home long enough to more than break even, refinancing your mortgage is a great idea. It's worth it.

For illustration purposes, let's say that your closing costs will amount to $6,000. Let's also say that you are going to save at least $300 every month from the refinancing agreement. In this scenario, you are going to break even in a period of twenty (20) months. That's less than two years.

Ratings Based on Our Criteria

A. **Simplicity:**
   I would not go as far as to say that this is simple because refinancing a mortgage can be very difficult and arduous. If you are unlucky, you might not even be able to secure a refinancing agreement.
   6/10

B. **Passivity:**
   The difference between the new interest rates and old interest rates definitely produces passive income.
   8/10

C. **Scalability:**
   This is almost impossible to scale unless you have more than one home. If you have several homes, you should get into real estate investing instead of trying to make money from refinancing.
   1/10

D. **Competitiveness:**
   Who would be competing to have your home refinanced? None. So competition in this arena is basically non-existent. You just have to be smart in negotiating your mortgage.
   10/10

Tips For Success

- Prepare your credit profile. This is the first thing that a financial company would look into if you were to shop around for a refinancing deal.

- Clearly identify your objectives. What's your end goal in refinancing? Is it to take equity or to reduce the monthly payments?

- Get appraisal. This provides you with a better understanding of how much your home is worth.

- Go over your application numerous times before submitting it. One mistake can ruin all of your chances.

- Use rising home prices to your advantage. You might want to consider tapping into your home's equity through a cash-out refinance.

- Compare APRs, not APYs. When looking around for a deal, you should pay more attention to quoted annual percentage rates (APR) than annual percentage yields (APY).

- Pick the right length. Just think about how long you want your mortgage to last before you enter into a refinance deal.

- Don't fall for no-cost refinance offers. There are always costs associated with a refinance deal. The company offering the no-costs deal is either lying or is trying to mislead you.

- Consider paying points. Sometimes, you can lower your interest rates by paying points. A point is usually equal to 1% of your loan value.

- Consider a rate lock. A rate lock is when you lock in an interest rate and cost structure with a particular lender regardless of whether the rate change from the period of the rate lock to the closing date.

Frequently Asked Questions and Answers

- What is a mortgage refinance?
    - Mortgage refinancing is the process of replacing your mortgage(s) on your property with a new mortgage, generally with different terms than the original mortgage. Mortgage refinancing will provide new money to the borrower, and used to pay off the original mortgage, usually with better mortgage terms

- What is the purpose of refinancing?
    - Common reasons for refinancing include taking advantage of lower interest rates, reducing monthly payments, converting adjustable rates to fixed rates, and choosing to cash-out.

- How much equity do I need to refinance?
    - It depends on the lender and the type of loan you originally acquired.

- How much does it cost to refinance?
    - The costs can range from two percent to five percent of the balance of the mortgage.

- Is it required to have good credit before you can refinance?
    - It depends on the new lender. However, keep in mind that there's an approval process with regards to refinancing. The better your credit status is, the better chances you have in getting a favorable refinancing deal.

- When should you consider going through mortgage refinancing?
    - It could be any of the following reasons. Your current mortgage has a rate that is above current market rates. You have an adjustable rate and you want to convert it into a fixed rate. You wish to improve cash flow by lowering your monthly payments.

- How much can I save if I refinance?

- It depends because very situation is different. There are a lot of factors that must be considered. It's advisable that you seek the help of a financial or loan consultant.

- Can I really reduce my payments by entering into a mortgage refinancing deal?
  - Yes because you can negotiate for a lower interest rate or for an extended maturity date.

- Can I refinance if I've had bad credit in the past?
  - It is definitely possible. The new lender will have to look into your employment history, income trend, as well as your debt and cash reserves.

- What are the closing costs involved in refinancing a mortgage?
  - Closing costs vary per lender and your mortgage type and your place of residence determine these. Closing costs may include lender fees, third-party fees, appraisals, and title insurance.

Myth Busters About Refinancing Your Mortgage

- You're supposed to be an expert. People always tend to assume that you should know how to refinance your home if you've been paying for it for too long. That's not always the case.

- Refinance applications require a lot of documents. The process is actually often faster and less of a hassle.

- That you need cash to cover closing costs. Most of the time, cash isn't necessary.

- That it's all about getting a lower rate. Lowering the rate isn't always the reason why people refinance their mortgage.

- That your current lender can offer you the best rates. Nope, that isn't always the case.

- That you haven't reached the break-even point of your current loan. You can still refinance if you haven't reached the break-even point.

- That you need 20% equity to refinance. This is not always the case. While loans with less than 20% equity may require mortgage insurance, you are still 100% eligible to apply for a refinance. Even with the addition of mortgage insurance, refinancing could still be a good move for you, particularly if it saves you money in the long run.

- That you won't save that much money by refinancing. You can save a lot of money by refinancing if you are smart about it.

Business #51

Building and Renting Email Lists

Most bloggers these days earn a good chunk of their revenue through email marketing. Whenever they have a new product to promote, they just send a single email to thousands of recipients; if even just a fraction of those who received the email followed through and made a purchase, that would be enough for the blogger/influencer to cash out and make a bit of income.

Aside from making money, having a mailing list will allow bloggers to interact with their audiences. For instance, after the promotional part of the email, bloggers could ask the recipients about their recent experiences with the website, like what could they do better, what topics they want to discuss, and a lot of other things. The information that you can get from replies to your emails will prove invaluable in making your blog site grow.

Creating an email list takes a lot of time and effort, something that most bloggers do not have. Most of them need an email list, but most of them are too busy coming up and creating fresh content that they no longer have any time to do anything else, and that is why renting out email lists is so in demand these days.

Why Rent email lists?

The reason most online businesses (be it bloggers, media websites, etc.) do not bother with the creation of their own email list is because they will only be using it once, or maybe even two times a year, depending on the frequency of their promotions. This does not warrant them spending a lot of their time building their own list, when they could just easily rent one and be done with it; and this is where you come in.

You will be the one who will create email lists, preferably in different niche markets, and then renting them out to people who need them immediately. It is a win-win situation for both parties; the client immediately has a large database of people he/she can send a promotional email to, and you, the renter, makes quite a bit of money in passive income.

How to Create an Email List

The absolute hardest part of creating an email list is finding the people who would want to join. If you are creating a targeted list then you need to know where your potential audiences like to hang out. Statistics have shown that women are most likely to spend a lot of time on Facebook, while men spend more time on YouTube. The great thing about Facebook and other social media websites is that they have “groups”, which are people who share the same passions. Just find the groups that is within your niche market and join as many of them as you can.

Now that you found where your potential list entries congregate, you need to prepare the ways in which you will be capturing them. One of the oldest, and yet still most effective methods of lead capturing is the classic opt-in page. This is an online page wherein you ask people to sign up with their email addresses. You can put opt-in pages anywhere in your website, but the most popular placements are in the landing page and in the ribbon menu of your website.

Okay, say that you have an opt-in page ready, how do you get people to sign up? Simple, you bribe them. Give them something of value that will make them want to sign up for your email list. For instance, you can give them discounts on merchandise, free content, anything that could get people’s attention and provide them with value. Examples of things that you can give to potential subscribers include ebooks, tutorial videos, and other goods that will not require you to spend money, and yet still provide value.

How to Monetize Your Email List

The best way to monetize your email list is to rent it out to website owners and companies whose niche market is the same as the people on your list. For instance, if the people on one of your lists are into automotive topics, look for clients in the same niche market, like say a producer of aftermarket parts. When you send an email blast to all of the recipients in your email listing, every one will receive the same email, and hopefully a good portion of them will reply in kind.

Ratings Based on Our Criteria

A) **Simplicity**
Creating an email list is not as simple as most people think. You need to create an opt-in portal, search for people who fit your niche market, and then persuade them to sign up for your email list.

5/10

B) **Passivity**
Once you have built a sizeable email list you can actually leave it at that. You just wait for clients who would want to rent your list for their marketing campaigns. This is as close to true passive income that you can get because you have the option to not put any more work on your list and just make money off of it.

8/10

C) **Scalability**
Email lists are definitely scalable. If you have one email list going, you can immediately start making another one, but on a different niche, so you have more bases covered. You can continue creating even more lists until you manage to cover as many different niche markets as you can.

8/10

D) **Competitiveness**
You will be up against quite a lot of competition, so you need to ensure the quality of your email list. There are surely a lot of people out there who have massive email listings that almost always ensure conversions, so you need to keep your price competitive to keep up with the others.

5/10

Tips For Success

- **Make targeted lists** – One way to make sure that your clients will be coming back to you is if they actually got conversions from your email lists. You can do this by providing your clients with an email list that caters to the kind of business your target has.
- **Create remarkable email content** – You want the readers of your email to opt-in to your list, right? Then you need to create content that is actually interesting and fun to read, not to mention informative.
- **Ask your readers to forward your emails to their friends and family** – Place a social sharing button in your emails and encourage your readers to share your emails to their friends and families. If you have established a level of trust with your readers, and if you make sharing your emails as hassle-free as possible, then they will not have any trouble at all when it comes to sharing your emails.
- **Create a "free" online tool or resource** – For instance, if you want to collect email addresses from people who like playing tabletop RPGs, then you can create a random fantasy name generator, which they can use for free if they sign up with their email addresses.
- **Use your social media accounts to hold contests** – A good way to get people to opt-in to your email list is by getting a sponsored post on any social network of your choosing and then ask them to send in their email addresses so they can join an online raffle. Make sure that the prize will actually make people want to join.
- **Shorten your lead capturing forms** – People are usually scared off when they see that they have to fill-up a lengthy form. Just limit the fields into a couple of spaces (Full name, date of birth, and email address), you can get more information out of them later if you need to.
- **Create a blog** – Creating a blog that requires people to sign in makes for a great email capture tool. Just make sure that your blog content is actually informative, fun to read, and provides worthwhile information.
- **Add engagement features to your online videos** – If you have a YouTube channel, and if you don't you really should look into making one, place hyperlinked "end cards" that appear at the end of your videos.

- **Ask website visitors for feedback** – At the bottom of your website, add a feedback link so that your website visitors can provide you with any criticism, praise, and anything else that they might want to tell you.
- **Add a hyperlink to your official email signature** – Adding a hyperlink to your official email signature will provide yet another avenue for potential lead generation.

Frequently Asked Questions and Answers

- **How do you get started?** – There are many ways that you can start building your email list from scratch. For instance, you can create a Call-to-Action that you can place after a blog post, or if you are a vlogger, ask your viewers to sign up before or after your video.
- **How much can you rent email lists?** – The cost of renting an email list is based on its CPM (cost per thousand; "M" is the Roman numeral for 1,000). Typically, for a targeted list that has 5,000 entries, you can charge around $400 for a consumer list, and $600 if it is a business list.
- **Why is renting email lists better than buying lists?** – First of all, not everyone has the time or energy to start their list from scratch. Secondly, the time they would spend growing their list could have been used in a more cost-effective manner.
- **Why is email list marketing effective?** – The biggest reason why it is so cost-effective is because it is, in fact, low cost. You only need an email list, and a program that will let you send thousands of emails at a time.
- **Do you need to send different emails to individual recipients?** – If you have a targeted email list then you can send just one email to everyone in your list. However, you can also group the members of your list depending on their niche, and send different emails to different groups.
- **How can I make people sign up to my list?** – There are many ways you can get people to sign up for your email list; you can email individual people asking for their basic information, nothing too over the top, just ask them to sign up, and they will receive a simple free gift from you.
- **Can people opt out of my lists?** – They should be able to. You have no right forcing people to be on your mailing list. It will be highly unethical for you to get people's emails without their permission.
- **How can you tell if people actually read your emails?** – You actually cannot tell if any people open your emails, much less read them. You just need to trust that at least some of the people in your mailing list actually takes the time to read your emails and a good portion of those actually go and buy the product.
- **How can I encourage people to join my list?** – There are many ways that you can convince people to join your list. For instance, you can offer them a free gift just for signing up, like an e-book or a video tutorial.
- **Where can I find people who'd want to rent my email list?** – You can post your email listings in online marketing forums, also, you can post your listing on eBay, Craigslist, and other online selling websites.

Myth Busters About Renting Emails

- **Using pop-ups to collect leads is passe** – Pop-ups are still here because they work. And they are now smarter and less intrusive because they are targeted. As long as you use pop-up ads wisely, they can gather leads.
- **You cannot collect emails using mobiles** – Although Google lowers your mobile site's ranking when its algorithm notices that you use pop-up ads. You just need to follow Google's Mobile SEO rules, so instead of using surprise pop-ups, use a click-trigger to cause the pop-ups to appear. Almost everyone and his brother now use a smartphone, it would be a shame not to make use of them.
- **Just asking people to sign up is okay** – It is not enough that you create a pop-up that asks people for their information. You need to entice people to make them want to sign up for your mailing list; you need to give them something of value, like a discount, free webinar registration, and ebooks are just some of the things of value that you can offer at no extra cost to you.

- **Being creative is better than being straightforward** – There is nothing wrong about being creative in your email lead collection, but going overboard will only confuse and confound your customers. Be straightforward with your message and your customers will be more than likely to help you out.
- **Popups chase people away** – This is not true, mainly because there are other pop-ups other than the aggressive ones that are annoying. There are ones that are non-intrusive at all, like using a click trigger, embedded pop-ups, and others.
- **Bigger lists are better** – This is not always the case. If you have a list containing 1,000 emails that are active and targeted, and another list containing 10,000 addresses that you just collected from anywhere that you can, and you have no idea how many of them are still active, or if they are actually genuine at all, the list with 1,000 email addresses would be much better.
- **List building costs money** – It will only cost money if you want to use expensive tools to build up your list quicker. However, you can also build an impressive email list using free online tools and a bit of patience. It might take a bit more time, but you will arrive at the same destination anyway.
- **You need to get as much info from the start** – Which kinds of online form would you more likely fill-up? One with three to four spaces, or one with a dozen or so questions? Of course, you'd choose the first option. Create pop-ups that would take less than a minute to completely fill-up, and just get more information out of your listing later using your emails.
- **You cannot build a list if you do not have emails prepared beforehand** – You do not necessarily have to start out with an elaborate automated messaging system in place. First of all, doing such a thing can be a frustrating affair, especially for a beginner like you. Secondly, automated systems take a long time to develop. Instead of waiting for your big system to shape up, prevent the loss of subscribers through inactivity by providing your subscribers with small automations with value.
- **Any kind of traffic is good traffic** – This is not always the case. Say you have a list containing 10,000 members, and you send out an email that discusses something obscure that only appeals to maybe 5% of them, that would be a horrible conversion rate. On the other hand, if you have a list containing targeted email addresses, even if there are only 2,000 members, you can get a better conversion rate and more profit.

Business #52

Testing Apps

Many app developers would not want to waste their money by releasing an app that consumers do not find user-friendly. Aside from getting scathing reviews from a bad app release, developers would like if some testers would try out their apps, provide helpful input and criticism, so that they can work out the kinks before the grand launch. Now, this is where you can come in and work as an app tester. There are actually companies that work as middlemen that helps developers find testers for their apps. If you want to work as an app tester and earn some money from the comfort of your home, you just need to sign up with these websites and check out what apps you can start testing.

Ratings Based on Our Criteria

A) Simplicity

All you need to do is sign up for an app testing account and then a beta copy of the app will be sent to you. You just need to examine the app and give your two cents about it.

7/10

B) Passivity

This is not exactly passive income because you will not be making money if you are not reviewing apps. On the other hand, it only takes a small amount of time for you to examine and rate an app, you can even test the apps during your lunch break at work and then send in your critiques and reports later in the evening.

5/10

C) Scalability

This is not that scalable at all. Of course, you can sign up on multiple app testing sites, so you can test multiple apps at the same time, but it will take a lot of your time and energy to review and critique multiple apps by yourself.

2/10

D) Competitiveness

Although there are many app testers out there, there are also quite a lot of app developers who would want people to do advance testing on their programs. There is more than enough room for everybody.

8/10

Tips For Success

- **Be objective** – Do not let your biases influence the way you test the apps. For instance, if you are tasked to test an astrology app, but you do not believe in things like that, do not let your own beliefs influence the way you test the app. Just concentrate of finding technical issues, set your beliefs aside.
- **Take your time and test everything that you can** – Testing apps takes time, you should not rush through the testing process because you might miss something important.
- **Communicate with the developer** – If there is a major flaw or security issue that you stumbled upon, you need to let the developer about the issue as soon as you can. Serious issues that could lead to the ultimate failure of the app needs to be addressed as soon as possible.
- **Learn about the common problems of certain kinds of apps** – The thing about programming errors is that they usually come up every time a developer wants to publish certain types of apps. For instance, for MMMORPGs, the persistent problem that happens during launch are server connection issues, so when

you review another MMORPG, especially if its from another developer, there is a chance that there will be server connection problems.

- **Keep a list** – List all of the problems that you encounter, write them down immediately so you don't forget them.
- **Consult your past testing projects** – As mentioned earlier, the same kind of errors come up from time to time in different apps. Take note of the most common errors that you found in the past and see if they are present in the app you're currently testing.
- **Confirm your findings** – Just because you found an anomaly, that does not mean it is a true issue. The only way to confirm it is to repeat the sequence of actions that you previously did and see if it happens again.
- **Be consistent; have a testing process** – When you test an app, you do not just randomly open and close tasks to find out if there are problems or not. You have to be systematic about it; have a uniform testing process that covers all the bases so you will not miss anything worth noting.
- **Keep a record of your past findings** – Always keep records of your past testing projects. Take note of what you did in the app to trigger the error. In other projects, you can repeat the same sequence to see if the error pops up there too.
- **Don't give up your integrity/be honest** – Even if you liked the products the developer made in the past, do not let that cloud your judgment and treat the app as you would any other.

Frequently Asked Questions and Answers

- **How much does it pay** – It depends on what kind testing is require by the client and how extensive the test will be.
- **How will I receive my payment** – Most companies use Paypal as a means of sending payments. If you do not have a Paypal account, you can easily make one for free.
- **What are the requirements to be a tester** – You just need to have a mobile device that is compatible with the apps that you will be testing. Also, you have to complete and pass the online assessment test.
- **Do I need to pay to join** – No, you should not pay for the opportunity to work, regardless of what industry it may be. If you are being asked to pay a registration fee then you can be sure that it is a scam.
- **When can I start testing** – The length of time depends on the company. Usually, a day or so after passing the assessment test they will receive an email that will tell them what to do next.
- **Do I need to know how to code** – No, you do not have to know programming at all to become a tester, you just need to have basic QA skills. Although, if you know how to code, you have the advantage of knowing what errors the app developer might have made and how to trigger the error.
- **Do I have to work at certain hours** – No, most companies only provide you with a particular length of time to finish reviewing an app; you can work any time that is convenient for you. How do I report my findings?
- **Where will I receive the apps** – The company will usually send the installer file to your email. You need to know how to install apps on your phone without using the Google Play Store or Apple Appstore.
- **Can I take more than one testing job** – Usually, review websites only allow one app per tester. However, there's nothing stopping you from registering at other testing websites so you can get other apps to review.
- **How do I make my reports** – The company will provide you with a template that you need to follow when writing your report.

Myth About Testing Apps

- **Testers are only involved before launch** – No, testing can also be done while the software is still in development. Some of the apps that you will be testing might not even have any pictures.
- **Testing is not technical and easy** – If you think that you will only be using the app and taking note of the things that you discovered then you are sorely mistaken. You need to follow a specific format when testing and reporting your findings.

- **Some people are just natural-born testers** – That's not true at all. You can learn how to become an effective app tester.
- **You only need to test the UI of the app** – There will be times when you have to test the app thoroughly, meaning you have to test all of the features of the app, even the ones that are embedded deep in the programming.
- **You will be testing fully developed apps** – There will be times when the app you will be testing is only half-finished, and the developer will only require you to test certain parts of the app.
- **It is possible to completely test an app** – No, as much as you want to, it is impossible for you to test an app completely.
- **A tested app is completely error free** – Not just because an app has been tested, that does not mean that it is completely bug-free, there will still be a couple of bugs that get through.
- **It is the tester's fault if there are errors left** – Even if there are bugs left in the app after launch, it is not the tester's fault that they're there. It is still ultimately the responsibility of the developer to make sure the app works right.
- **Testers are responsible for the quality of the product** – No, the responsibility of the tester is to check if the app is user-friendly, but the task of quality control is still in the hands of the developer.
- **Your only task is to discover bugs in the code** – No, you will also check if the app is user-friendly or not. For instance, are the buttons large enough for adult fingers, are they responsive, are the texts easy to read, etc.

Business #53

Review Music

There are many independent musicians out there who do not have a professional producer and a team of sound engineers to tell them if what they have is any good or not. This is why many of them use online music review services to help them get honest to goodness criticisms and feedback so they can hone their music better.

You can become one of these online music reviewers, and the great thing about it is that you do not have to quit your day job. You can critique and judge other people's music on your spare time, and earn a good chunk of change at the same time.

To become a music reviewer, you just need to create an account in one of the many music review websites; one of the most popular these days is slicethepie.com. Once you have created an account, you can start browsing their music library and then choose the songs that you want to review. The amount of money you will earn will depend on the rates that the site will provide.

Ratings Based on Our Criteria

A) **Simplicity**
There is nothing too technical about judging music, you just need to point out the things that you liked or didn't like. You do not have to criticize every minute detail, just the ones that you notice.
8/10

B) **Passivity**
Surprisingly, music reviewing is actually a pretty good way to earn passive income, but this does not apply to all companies. Some online review companies, like sliceofthepie.com, offer referral services, meaning that if you recruit other reviewers (they need to use your referral code upon sign up), and they pass the assessment test, you stand to earn up to 10% of their earnings on top of what you earn in the company. So, if you can manage to wrangle up 10 friends and family members who love music, you can essentially double your earnings.
8/10

C) **Scalability**
Thanks to the referral programs provided by some online companies, you can scale up your earning potential by recruiting as many new reviewers as you can. You can actually make more money recruiting reviewers than actually reviewing music yourself, that is if you have a knack for recruiting people.
8/10

D) **Competitiveness**
There are lots of people who earn extra income by reviewing music, fortunately there are also lots of websites that offer this kind of service, and there are always musicians who want feedback for their music.
7/10

Tips For Success

- **Be objective** – You should not let your personal preferences affect your judgment. For instance, if you do not really like country music, but you need to review one, set aside your dislike and just give it a listen. Judge the music according to its merits and shortcomings, not according to your tastes.
- **Be honest and truthful** – Do not sugarcoat your critiques, the clients actually like it when they get honest reviews, because that gives them ideas on what they need to work on. If you do not give an honest assessment, the other reviewers will, and the client will get confused as to why you differ in opinion from the others.

- **Give detailed explanations** – Don't just say that you did not like a certain part of the song, you need to explain why you did not like it. For instance, instead of just saying that you did not like the introduction, you should explain it in more detail, like you did not like that the intro took almost a minute before actually getting into the song.
- **Explore different genres of music** – You should not just stick with just one genre of music, especially if you want to be a music reviewer. You need to force yourself to listen to other genres of music if need be. You do not have to necessarily love all genres, you just need to have some appreciation of them. For instance, you do not need to love all country music, but you should at least like a couple of them so you know what makes a good country song.
- **Start writing the moment the song starts** – It is best to give your reactions right at the moment. Have a pen and paper ready before you play the music so you can write down your reactions the moment that you get them. It is better to give your criticisms on the first time you hear the song because listeners will do the same. You can give the song another listen just to confirm your initial judgment.
- **Critique every part of the song** – You need to judge the whole song, not just certain parts of it. Give feedback about the music, the melody, the lyrics, and other things that you might have an opinion on. It is most likely that you will be provided with template that you need to base your reports on, and you might also find the criteria for judging there as well.
- **Give your review a proper structure** – As mentioned earlier, the company will usually provide you with a template that you need to follow when writing your reports. If not, you should create your own template, one that is complete and organized. You need to provide space where you can place your thoughts on the different parts of the and aspects of the song.
- **Check your biases** – Just because you do not like the message of the song, that does not mean it is automatically bad. You need to keep your personal biases in check when judging music. You need to be objective, base your decision on the music's merits, and don't let your personal beliefs influence you.
- **Be careful when giving really high scores** – If there is a song that you really like, but do be careful not to give perfect, or near perfect marks. If you can, check the score that other reviewers have given the song, or at least find the average rating that it got so far. If you are really impressed, and you can justify your grade accordingly, then go ahead. If you just really liked the song, but you cannot explain why, just give a score that is a bit above the average.
- **Don't worry about hurting the artists' feelings** – It is not your job to coddle the artists; you are there to provide constructive criticism for their work. If you do not give them the marks that they deserve, then they are just wasting their money on you. Be honest and blunt with your judgment, you will actually be helping the artists more when you do this rather than being a "yes man".

Frequently Asked Questions and Answers

- **Where do I sign up** – There are many online websites that provide music review services. You just need to sign up for a free account, and then take the assessment test so that they can find out if you are actually fit to become a music reviewer. Do not worry, the test is usually not technical, it's just to find out if you have the right QA skills.
- **How much money will I make** – It depends on the service. Most of the time, there are different rates depending on the song and what kinds of criticisms that the artists would like to get.
- **How will I get paid** – Most of these services use Paypal as a payment processor. Do not worry if you do not have a Paypal account, it's easy to set up a new account, and best of all, it's free.
- **How do I create reviews** – When you passed the company's assessment test, usually within 24 hours you will gain access to their database. You just need to pick a song that you want to review and then download the file on your computer or smartphone. The company will provide you with a template that you need to follow when making a review.
- **Do I have to work at a particular time** – No, you can work at any time that is convenient for you. The only catch is that you need to finish the review within the specified amount of time.

- **Will I be reviewing songs by popular singers** – No, popular artists have their own team that does the critiquing of new songs. You will mainly be reviewing the works of independent artists, newcomers at the scene, and semi-professional recording artists. However, you can never tell if the song and artist that you reviewed will hit it big someday.
- **Can I pick the genre of music I review** – Usually the company will let you pick the song and music genre to review. However, there might be some companies that will randomly assign songs for you to review.
- **How long does it take to review music** – It depends on you; it might take you less than ten minutes, or it might take half an hour. Don't worry about the deadlines of the reports, they are usually very reasonable.
- **Do I need to have theoretical knowledge about music** – No, but it does help if you know a little about music theory so you can add a bit of technical knowledge into your reviews.
- **Do I need to have a musical background** – No, you do not have to be a musician yourself if you want to be a music reviewer. You just need to have a love for music, and a discerning ear for what sounds good and what does not.

Myth About Reviewing Music

- **You will be reviewing unreleased tracks from your favorite artists** – No, established popular musical artists have their own teams that do the reviewing for them. The bulk of the music that you will be providing feedback for are from indie acts.
- **You need to be a musician yourself to review music** – No, you do not need to be in the music industry in any way if you want to become a music reviewer. You just need to have an ear for what sounds good, and you know what might be popular to today's crowd.
- **You need to take the feelings of the musician into consideration** – No, this is the one time that you must rein in your empathy a bit because you really need to be objective and honest when giving your opinion. If you hold back because you are afraid of hurting the feelings of the artists then you will be of no help to them; harsh, yet honest criticisms will help them improve.
- **You will be reviewing music that you don't really like** – You usually have the option of choosing the genre of music to review, but it would actually be better for you if you review music that you are not really fond of. Reviewing other genres will open up your mind, making you more appreciative of different kinds of music.
- **You will be reviewing completed songs** – Not all the time. There might be times when you will be giving your thoughts on just the melody, with the lyrics of the song only half done.
- **You need to refer other people into the site to earn money** – No, you can earn without referring anybody to sign up with the site. However, you are missing out on some serious earning potential if you didn't recruit anyone.
- **You can make a decent living reviewing music** – Again, if you are not referring anyone else to the site, reviewing music is just a means of getting some additional side income; not enough to actually pay all the bills.
- **You can cash out any time** – This is not always the case. Most companies put a limit before reviewers can cash out. Most companies maintain that you need to earn at least $10 before you can cash out.
- **The artists know who reviewed their music** – No, all of the music reviewers can remain anonymous if they want to be. There are some people who do not care if the artist knows who they are, but for the sake of safety, most music review companies hide the names and personal information of their reviewers.
- **Your opinions are always correct** – Do not be surprised when other reviewers give drastically different marks on a song. Judging the merits of a piece of music is always subjective, so your opinions will most likely be different from other reviewers, but that does not necessarily mean that you're wrong or right. As long as you explain your thought process, your opinions will always be valid.

Business #54

Webinars

What is a webinar? Short for Web-based Seminar, webinars are like lectures that are transmitted online using a kind of video conferencing program. What makes webinars different from online classes? Webinars are always done live, and they also allow the participants to interact with the lecturer in real time. For instance, before the webinar officially starts, the lecturer can provide files and documents so that the participants can easily follow the lecture later.

Webinar programs nowadays also have additional features, like recording the live stream so that you can publish it later on YouTube, so that more people can gain access to your lectures, albeit without the interactivity.

How do your earn from webinars, you ask? There are actually a number of ways that you can earn money by creating webinars, and it is actually a nice way to generate passive income if you play your cards right. For instance, offer products or services that are related to the subject of your webinar to the attendees. If you are great at sales, you can pretty much convince the other people who are behind the camera lens that what you are peddling is actually beneficial for them.

Ratings Based on Our Criteria

A) Simplicity

Creating webinars is a highly-technical task. First of all, you need to be somewhat of an expert on the subject of your lecture. Second, you need to have excellent public speaking skills. And third, you need to have at least some semblance of production value (sets, backdrops, any background that relates to your lecture).

5/10

B) Passivity

There are many ways you can generate passive income using webinars. First, there's the profit from the sales of products you pitched during your webinar. Second, you can earn ad revenue when you post your videos on your personal YouTube channel. The second option might take a bit of work, but there is much potential there.

9/10

C) Scalability

The more webinars you make the more chances of earning passive income you will get. Not only will you get commissions from the sales of the products that you promote during your webinar, you will also earn a lot of ad revenue when a lot of people view the webinar recordings in your YouTube channel.

8/10

D) Competitiveness

There are many people who make webinars, but only a few of them are actually so popular. Unless you are a celebrity, or at the very least have a sizeable following, you will have a hard time collecting passive income from your

7/10

Tips For Success

- **Create a usable outline** – Before you jump into the lecture proper, you need to prepare an outline for the session. This will help you make sure that all of the important talking points are covered and that you do not stray too far away from the topic at hand.
- **Show, don't tell** – Instead of just talking your way through the entire lecture, make use of visual aids and maybe a couple of videos to aid your lecture. Don't just post a huge wall of text and then read through it,

that is not only boring, it is also somewhat insulting to the intellect of your webinar attendees; they do not need someone else to read the lecture handouts for them.

- **Have slides cycle while you talk** – You need to make full use of your and your attendee's time by multi-tasking; while you are explaining some of the finer details of the topic, have slides that visualize what you're talking about appear next to you on the screen.
- **Use graphics liberally and contextually** – If your attendees wanted to read huge walls of text then they should just read an online article. However, the reason why they chose to attend your webinar is so they can get an easier explanation of the topic. So don't drown your presentation with text, use graphics (graphs, charts, photographs, etc.) to explain the topic further.
- **Don't be too detail-oriented** – No one needs to know all the details about the topic, they just need a concise explanation of the important things. For instance, no one needs to know how internal combustion engines work if they just want to learn how to drive a car.
- **Use crystal clear audio, and have a non-distracting background music running in the background** – There's nothing quite as distracting as dead air; that space in your lecture where you are still thinking about what to say next. That couple of seconds can derail the whole lecture, so to prevent this from happening, have some sort of faint background music playing in your background.
- **Provide interactivity** – Your attendees will learn a whole lot more if you let them interact with you during the duration of the lecture. Enable the chat box so they can send in questions if there is something that is unclear. Give your audience enough time to respond if needed.
- **Minimize the use of colloquialisms** – It is very likely that you will have attendees that come from different countries, and not all of them are familiar of your local colloquialisms, so limit your use of them, or do not use them entirely if possible.
- **Discussions should always be about the topic and does not stray** – Do not stray away from the actual topic of the discussion. It's alright to waiver from time to time, but do steer it back on track as soon as you can.
- **Have someone help you moderate the chat** – It is hard to keep up with all the questions sent by the attendees and provide a lecture at the same time. Have someone moderate the chat box for you and take note of the more relevant questions and then feed them to you for answers.

Frequently Asked Questions and Answers

- **How long do webinars usually last** – On average, webinars can last from 45 minutes to an hour. Speakers would usually give a talk for half an hour and then have a 10 to 15 minute break so that the lecturer and the attendees can rest a bit.
- **What time do they start** – It depends on the time zone of the lecturer. Usually it happens during the mid-morning or early-afternoon in the lecturer's time zone, so if you are from the other side of the world, you might need to wait until it is night time to attend the webinar.
- **Where can I take the class from** – Anywhere you have access to the internet is acceptable, there are also no real restrictions about where or when you need to attend the webinar.
- **Will there be a quiz after? And how will I take it?** – It depends, most webinars do not require the attendees to take quizzes, but if the webinars are a part of a certification program then there might be an online quiz that will be presented after the examination.
- **Do the viewers need to have microphones** – No, the attendees can interact with the lecturer via the chat box; using voice chat would be very disruptive.
- **How can the viewers interact with the speaker** – The attendees of the webinar can interact with the lecturer via the chat box provided by the webinar app. They just need to post questions in the chatbox, and wait for the lecturer to respond.
- **Is interaction required** – No, but it would help the attendees more if they would interact with the lecturer. For instance, if you did not clearly understand something, you can ask clarifying questions to the lecturer who will hopefully reply immediately and make adjustments going forward.

- **What kinds of questions are acceptable** – It depends on the topic and the discretion of the lecturer. However, you should refrain from making personal attacks at the lecturer, doing so will be a good way for you to get kicked out of the webinar.
- **Do you need anything when taking a webinar** – It is best to have a pen and paper ready to write down the important points, and also to jot down any questions that you might want to ask later.
- **What's the difference between webinars and online training** – Webinars are always done live and in real time, which is why if you are living in the opposite side of the world as the lecturer then you might need to wait until the wee hours of the night. On the other hand, online training videos are prerecorded, so you have no real time interactivity with the lecturer.

Myth About Webinars

- **Webinars costs an arm and a leg** – No, there are actually a lot of affordable webinar applications out there that you can use. Also, you do not need to have an elaborate set to create a compelling webinar. In fact, if your living room is neat enough, or if there is a quiet part of your house, they can be viable places to start a webinar.
- **Webinars are too hard to make** – Not really, you just need to prepare everything a couple of important things. You do not need a fancy camera, a smartphone camera would be good enough. You also need a webinar app installed in your laptop. Lastly, you need to prepare the lecture that you will be presenting to your attendees.
- **You have learned all you need about hosting a webinar from a class you took years ago** – Not really, there have been many changes that have happened in the world of online marketing, and even webinars are not immune to these changes. If you want to stay ahead of the pack, you need to keep your webinar knowledge up to date.
- **Webinars have become passe** – On the contrary, webinars have become even more popular today as more people now have access to high-speed internet, and they can even access the internet on their phones.
- **Webinars are just for marketing only** – No, the primary purpose of webinars is to inform others, making a profit is just a by-product.
- **Webinars should always be live** – Not necessarily. If someone does not have the time to catch the live webinar, they can still watch the recorded version later on the lecturer's YouTube channel.
- **Webinars with compelling video and audio are sure to succeed** – Compelling media does make a presentation look good, but they are not the key for a professional-looking webinar. The success of the webinar lies on the host and the quality of the subject matter.
- **You cannot use webinars to peddle products** – It is actually one of the best ways to plug your affiliate products if you have any. Some online marketers use webinars as one of their primary means of driving up their sales.
- **Social media is the only way to drive webinar attendance** – Social media is one of the main ways to drive up webinar attendance, but it is not the only method. You can invite other people to participate through sending out emails through your distribution list, or by offering the webinar as a free gift for signing up for your other marketing plans.
- **You need to be an expert to make a webinar** – Not really, but you do need to have knowledge about the topic that you will be discussing. For instance, if you want to do a webinar series about common car troubleshooting, you do not have to be a mechanical engineer, you can be a hobbyist who has years of experience working on different cars.

Business #55

Mobile App Theme Design

Before you can even start writing a single line of code to create a mobile app, you need to have it designed first. Having a design on hand will serve as a sort of roadmap for the developers; because you already know what it should look like, you just need to write the code to make it so.

However, not all developers have a keen eye for design. If they leave the design up to them, there is a chance that even if the app is useful, no one would use it because it is poorly designed. This is where you come in; you will be the one presenting your designs to mobile app developers so they have something to start from.

You post advertisements on eBay, Craigslist, and other online retailing sites. However, you can do better by posting ads in forums sites that discuss mobile app development.

Ratings Based on Our Criteria

A) **Simplicity**

If you are a creative person then designing app themes might be second nature for you. However, if you are not, then you might need a bit of practice.

5/10

B) **Passivity**

There are apps that charge extra for additional themes, you can submit your themes for these sites and you will get a percentage of the profits if anyone buys your theme.

6/10

C) **Scalability**

If you can manage to pass a lot of app themes to their respective storefronts then there is a chance that you might get passive income from them. However, the chances of making enough sales of app themes is quite low.

5/10

D) **Competitiveness**

Because app theme programs are commonplace, there are quite a lot of app theme designers out there who, like you, want to make money from their designs.

7/10

Tips For Success

- **The design should be responsive** – This means that the design should be viewable on portrait or landscape orientation. Not everyone likes to use their smartphones in portrait mode, some actually want to have a wider screen so they choose to use their devices on landscape mode most of the time.
- **Keep it simple** – No one finds a complicated design appealing, especially in a mobile app. If there is very limited space, overcrowding it with features will make it unusable. Keep your theme design simple, and easy to understand. Design it for the use of others, not just for yourself.
- **Keep it neat** – Do not clutter the space with a lot of unnecessary details. Bring the main features to the front, and embed the others underneath them. A clean-looking interface will make using the app less strenuous.
- **Keep text to a minimum** – Do not use the full screen just to display texts. If you need to provide explanations for certain features, use a small text box with a brief yet concise content.

- **Update consistently** – You should not ignore any feedback that customers throw your way, especially the ones that are critical of your work. Use them to fix and improve upon your earlier design. Provide regular updates and bug fixes to your design until you no longer receive any reports.
- **Give the people what they want** – You should design the app according to the needs and wants of the consumers, not just for yourself. If you think the design looks good, but other people do not agree with you, and they explain why, then you should make the necessary changes.
- **Follow the guidelines set by Google and Apple** – If you want the app listed in these two major app repositories, you need to make sure that all of your applications follow their design guidelines.
- **Limit the use of typefaces** – Using different typefaces might look cool, but using too much makes the design look cluttered. You should use just one or two typefaces at a time, this will give the app a sense of uniformity.
- **Be clever when using colors** – You should study a bit of color theory. Different kinds of colors incite different emotions, so you should use the right kinds of colors depending on the kind of app you will be designing for.
- **Be consistent with all the pages** – Do not use different design themes in the different parts of the app. Be consistent with the design all throughout the app.

Frequently Asked Questions and Answers

- **Do I have to be a graphic designer to create app themes** – Not necessarily, you just need to have a sense of design.
- **Do I need to know how to code** – No, there are actually apps that you can use to create themes. These programs already have intuitive UIs that make designing app themes easier.
- **Do I need to get training** – There are classes that you can take to learn how to make effective designs. However, if you have a good sense of design, you can probably start without any training whatsoever.
- **How will I get paid** – If you will be working directly with the developer, it will depend on your arrangements. Usually, you can charge 50% to 70% up front and the remainder upon final submission of the design.
- **Will I only be designing for mobile apps** – Most of the clients will be developers of mobile apps, but there are times when you will also be tasked to design websites (mobile and traditional)
- **How much will I get paid** – It depends on the complexity and scale of the design. If you will be designing a web site that is a dozen or so pages deep, you can charge a substantial amount.
- **What apps can I use to create app designs** – The great thing about app design is that you do not have to start from scratch; you do not even need to know HTML to create your designs. There are some that are as easy as choosing backgrounds, screen elements, and others.
- **Can I resell the designs that other clients did not like** – Yes, you own the right to the designs, so you can sell them to other clients if you so wish. You just need to make adjustments so that the design will suit the needs of your new client.
- **Can I copy other people's designs** – No, blatant plagiarism is frowned upon. However, you can take inspiration from the designs of others, like taking some design elements (borders, screen elements, typography, layout, etc.) and tweaking them a bit to make them your own.
- **How long will it take to finish a design** – Again, this will depend on the complexity of your design. However, most clients will give you more than enough time to work on your design before you even pass the first draft.

Myth About Mobile App Theme Design

- **Mobile users are always in a rush and are easily distracted** – This is an unfair generalization. There are many mobile users who actually want to use their devices to read articles and other literature. You should not oversimplify your app design to the point that there are only icons in a page.

- **Mobile apps and websites must be "lite"** – Not really. Mobile users want full-featured apps too. Lite apps are just for those who want to save on their data plans.
- **Everybody needs a mobile site** – Everybody does not really "need" mobile sites, but they would definitely benefit by having one. However, I'm sure that there are some companies that do not need mobile sites, but they are few and far in between.
- **Mobile apps are better than mobile websites** – They are equally beneficial, however, depending on the browser used, mobile websites usually load faster.
- **User experience is the same as user interface** – No. The user interface is enclosed under the umbrella of total user experience. It's like this: A horrible UI means a horrible UX, but a horrible UX does not necessarily mean that the UI is bad.
- **Users do not scroll to the bottom** – Many designers assume that mobile users rarely scroll all the way to the bottom of a page, so they cram as much information in the first page as possible. However, a cluttered UI makes people want to uninstall the app. Design the theme in such a way that you provide just enough information on the front page, so that the user will want to scroll down to learn more.
- **The users like the same things you do** – Just because you like your design, that does not necessarily mean others will too. Before submitting your design for approval, ask your friends and family what they think about your design.
- **Design means making it look good** – If an app is designed well, not only will it look good, it will function well too. Good aesthetics is secondary to providing a pleasant user experience.
- **The design needs to be original** – This can be very difficult, especially for people like you who are newcomers in the industry. Although outright copying the designs of other people, you could "take inspiration" from them instead. You do not have to copy everything, just some of the details that make them great.
- **Using stock photos will make your site more appealing** – Using stock photos to take care of the white space in the app or website does little to add value to the website, this is especially true when the stock photos are only remotely related to the contents.

Conclusion

Before anything else, I would like to thank you for reading this book up to this point. That only shows that you are truly serious in pursuing opportunities that will earn you decent passive income. Being serious about it is a good start. It also prepares you in developing the right mindset. As I've mentioned in the beginning of this book, having the right mindset is crucial to your success. Most of the people who fail in this journey do so because they didn't have the right mental approach. They were lazy. They got discouraged too easily. They didn't have patience. If you truly read this book and follow it up by implementing the tips and strategies discussed within, I am confident that you are going to reach your passive income goals.

Furthermore, I want to share with you something that I find terribly sad. Once people start reading a book, they typically only read 10 percent of it before they give up or forget about it. Only 10 percent. What's sad about this is that from this statistic, we can see that very few people actually follow through on what they commit to (at least when it comes to reading). The reason for this is harsh but understandable: most people are not willing to hold themselves accountable. People "want" and "want" all day, but very few actually have the fortitude to put in the work.

So what's my point? First, I am trying to tell you that if you're reading these words, you are a statistical anomaly (and I am grateful for you). But here's the kicker: in order to become successful as a result of this book, you are going to have to be in the .1 percent. You need to take action.

So What's Next?

Now that you are fully aware of the various opportunities that you can explore in your attempt to generate passive income, what's the next step? Well, it's time to pull up your sleeves and get to work. It's time to take action. It's time to fire up that laptop and start getting things done. Many aspiring online entrepreneurs will never achieve their goals because they never get started. Don't be one of these dreamers. You have to take action.

I'll tell you right now that getting started is going to be difficult and often confusing. But that is part of the game. As the saying goes, the city of Rome wasn't built in one day. Generating a good amount of passive income takes time and hours of hard work. It can be weeks, months, or even years before you get to see some consistent revenue coming your way. This is why throughout this book, I've always reiterated the values of patience, determination, and discipline. If you don't have these attributes, your journey can be easily cut short by the smallest setback.

Others Did It, So Can You

There are a lot of people out there making decent passive income using one or more of the ways discussed in this book. Although most of them are doing it part-time, there are those who have turned it into a full-time gig i.e. they make 100% of their income from their online businesses. It's not uncommon for a blogger or affiliate marketer to be making six figures a year. Some even make six figures a month. The bottom line here is that it's really possible to create a comfortable income stream from a passive source. If others can, then you can as well.

My last piece of advice for you is this: "Set your goals and don't stop until you achieve them." Don't let anything or anyone try to discourage or bring you down. Just focus on those goals and keep on working and hustling towards them. That's what most successful entrepreneurs would do. Work hard, work smart, and be patient. These are the keys to achieving your goals. It doesn't matter if these are short-term or long-term goals. I wish you the very best of luck!

The End

Thank you very much for taking the time to read this book. I tried my best to cover as many ways to earn passive income as I could. If you found it useful please let me know by leaving a review on Amazon! Your support really does make a difference and I read all the reviews personally so can I understand what my readers particularly enjoyed and then feature more of that in future books.

I also pride myself on giving my readers the best information out there, being super responsive to them and providing the best customer service. If you feel I have fallen short of this standard in any way, please kindly email me at **michael@michaelezeanaka.com** so I can get a chance to make it right to you. I wish you all the best with your journey towards financial freedom!

Lightning Source UK Ltd.
Milton Keynes UK
UKHW031838090223
416723UK00007B/327